CW00496500

SURREY AIR
IN THE SEC
WORLD WAR

To Colin
with all Best Wishes
for 2 May 2003
Ralph.

SURREY AIRFIELDS IN THE SECOND WORLD WAR

Len Pilkington

COUNTRYSIDE BOOKS
NEWBURY, BERKSHIRE

First published 1997
© Len Pilkington 1997

Reprinted, with revisions 1998, 2001

COUNTRYSIDE BOOKS
3 Catherine Road
Newbury, Berkshire

ISBN 1 85306 433 5

To view our complete range of books,
please visit us at
www.countrysidebooks.co.uk

The cover painting is by Colin Doggett and shows Mustangs of 414
(AC) Squadron leaving Croydon airfield in 1942.

Map of the Surrey airfields by Trevor Yorke

Designed by Mon Mohan

Produced through MRM Associates Ltd., Reading
Typeset by Techniset Typesetters, Merseyside
Printed by Woolnough Bookbinding Ltd., Irthlingborough

CONTENTS

INTRODUCTION

Surrey was always destined to become a front line county during the Second World War because of its proximity to London. But the county was no stranger to the aeroplane and indeed was already rich in aviation history well before the clouds of war gathered and increased in menace during the 1930s.

The association goes back to the first balloon ascent from Hurst Park on 1st May 1785 by James Sadler, using a hydrogen balloon which landed on the Isle of Grain. In 1902 Stanley Spencer flew a powered balloon or 'airship' from the Crystal Palace. It covered a distance of 22 miles, proving controlled flight was possible. In Germany the design of similar machines was already well advanced under the direction of Count Ferdinand von Zeppelin.

It was now thought that the struggle for flight would be won by these ships of the air but in 1903 the Wright Brothers in America demonstrated that powered flight by a heavier than air machine was possible and things were soon to change. In 1908 Alliott Verdon Roe made the first powered flight in England from Brooklands. From then on that site became the Mecca of aerialists who rapidly produced a succession of aeroplane designs. In 1909 Frenchman Louis Bleriot flew the Channel and the future of the aeroplane was firmly established. Germany exploited the military potential of the Zeppelin airships and produced many battle squadrons, but in England the newly formed Royal Flying Corps concentrated on the aeroplane. They needed landing grounds, and it is the story of the development of these airfields or aerodromes in the county and the part they played in the Second World War that is told here. The lives of civilians in a county at war are also recounted, with first-hand accounts of the bombing attacks that claimed so many lives.

The reader will no doubt observe that the airfields included are those which were within the geographical county boundary which existed at the time. From 1965, Croydon became a London borough and Gatwick was absorbed into Sussex.

It is hoped that reading these chapters will encourage the reader to delve further into the fascinating history of Surrey's airfields, and perhaps experience the magical atmosphere of the Brooklands museum.

Len Pilkington

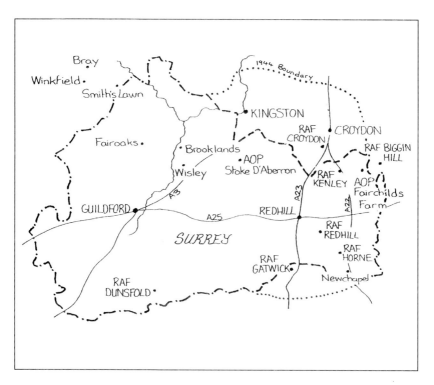

Map showing the airfields in Surrey, 1944.

I
SETTING
THE SCENE

When the First World War ended in 1918, Lloyd George's government began to dismantle the newly formed Royal Air Force, which had evolved from the Royal Flying Corps created in 1912. General Smuts' recommendation in 1917 that a strong, independent force should be maintained at all costs was ignored. By 1920 the 188 operational squadrons had been reduced to 25, with only a few for home defence.

Over the following years disagreements over the future of Britain's air force continued. In military circles there was great pressure to split the RAF back into its original army and navy components but fortunately this was prevented by the acceptance by Winston Churchill, for the government, of a report written by Sir Hugh Trenchard, Chief of Air Staff, outlining a plan for the continuance of an independent air force. The report advocated a provision of 33 operational squadrons, to be increased to 55 by 1923 for home defence.

The process of rebuilding the RAF was slow and in 1926 it became part of the Air Defence of Great Britain, a body set up to look into all aspects of defence. In 1929 Sir Hugh Trenchard retired after laying the foundations of the modern air force, launching the training facilities at Cranwell and Halton and forming the Auxiliary Air Force. Unfortunately, only 38 squadrons had yet been formed.

The expansion of the RAF was affected by a succession of delays by various governments, mainly for economic reasons, but in Germany no such restrictions were in force. A surreptitious build-up of military strength had begun under many guises. Pilots were being trained secretly in Lipetsk in Russia as early as 1924, and also in Germany under the pretence of glider flying. Civil aircraft were being produced that could quickly convert to military use, and when Hitler came to power in 1933 this upsurge rapidly accelerated.

Some progress was being made in Britain and 1931 saw the first results of the expansion programme here with the upgrading of certain airfields, including Kenley which was improved so as to provide a permanent base for two fighter squadrons. Hitler's rise to power, Germany's repudiation of the League of Nations, and the realisation by the British government that Germany was building a secret air force, prompted the introduction of another expansion scheme with a target of 75 Home Defence squadrons. This meant more airfields would be needed and the newly formed Air Ministry Works Directorate was given the job of designing and overseeing the work.

The political situation steadily worsened. Hitler introduced conscription and in 1936 occupied the Rhineland, a military buffer zone, in direct violation of the Versailles Treaty. He also defiantly made public acknowledgement of the existence of the Luftwaffe. Italy invaded Abyssinia and several RAF squadrons were tied up in Aden and Egypt keeping an eye on the situation out there.

The RAF now had its most crucial reconstruction in its short history. It was realised that one man could not command and administrate such a rapidly growing service and in 1936 it was therefore split into its functional parts, each one a separate command, thereby dissolving the old Air Defence of Great Britain structure. The result was the formation of Fighter Command, Bomber Command, Coastal Command, Training Command and Maintenance Command, with Balloon and Reserve Commands to follow. Further targets were set for growth to 112 squadrons by 1937.

In 1938, with units of the Luftwaffe flying with the Condor Legion in Spain, Germany marched into Austria and seemed likely to invade Czechoslovakia. France and Britain threatened war if this took place, but neither country was ready for war and a compromise was reached during the Munich Crisis. The uneasy peace was not to last and a year later Hitler had invaded Poland and war had been declared by Britain and France.

Surrey airfields were to play an important part in the coming conflict, as they had in the First World War, and their growth and development during the inter-war years mirrored developments in both civilian and military flying.

Early on in the First World War Mr H. F. Locke-King, the owner of the motor racing track at Brooklands, offered the site to the nation for the duration and the Royal Flying Corps took it over as an Air Acceptance Park, the first aerodrome in the county. It was immediately ready to receive aircraft from the manufacturers prior to squadron service and formed No 2 Home Defence Squadron. The unit commenced training pilots whilst Vickers, Sopwith and Martinsyde continued to design and build aircraft. As the war continued, the search for aircraft production units and suitable flying fields went on. Flat, open spaces with good communications, such as sports grounds and race tracks, were considered suitable and Hurst Park was the first to be taken over as an Air Acceptance Park for machines built to the west of London.

In the early days the full potential of the aeroplane had not been realised and the balloon was still considered the ultimate offensive flying weapon. In Surrey training schools were opened for army and navy personnel at Wormwood Scrubs Airship Station, a preliminary school for RNAS officers for service in captive balloons and dirigible airships ('blimps'). Roehampton polo ground was the RFC training ground for Kite balloon observers and Hurlingham, a noted pre-war ballooning centre, was used for certification flights for RFC and RNAS personnel.

In 1915 the German Zeppelins commenced their reign of terror with air raids over towns and cities in England and in May that year London was attacked from the air for the first time. Although the raids were not entirely unexpected there were no contingency plans for defence, and what defence there was consisted of a couple of three-inch naval guns and a dozen smaller weapons, with the Home Defence squadrons (mainly Be2Cs) night flying in the vain hope of spotting a raider. From the first raid Brooklands' aircraft were in action but with no success. Defences did improve, but it was not until 2nd September 1916 when Lieutenant Leefe-Robinson, VC, shot down the Schutte-Lanz airship at Cuffley in Hertfordshire with the new incendiary ammunition that the fate of the airships was sealed.

A new threat emerged on 28th November 1916 when a lone German aeroplane, in broad daylight and unchallenged, bombed London. In May 1917 large-scale attacks by twin-engined Gothas began and on 13th June four Gothas reached London, again in daylight and unchallenged, and killed 162 people. After another attack on 7th July, public outcry demanded action. The organisation and co-ordination of the London Defence Area by Brigadier General E. Ashmore stopped the raids, only for them to restart in September by the Gotha and Giant

Reisen bombers. Ashmore again improved defences and when a Bristol fighter from Biggin Hill, using the first ground to air radio communication, intercepted and shot down a Gotha, the raids petered out.

The search for new sites for Home Defence aerodromes had intensified and in the spring of 1916, Manor Farm and New Barn Farm at Beddington near Croydon were purchased. A squadron of Be2Cs arrived from Hounslow and were soon in action. In 1917 further land was acquired on Kenley Common along with two adjacent farms, New Barn and Waterhouse, for use as an Air Acceptance Park. Temporary canvas Bessoneaux hangars were erected while the permanent Belfast type were being built. Kenley was very busy erecting and test-flying aircraft before delivery to squadrons, and so took little part in the defence of London. Brooklands' main function became the training of pilots, but it was also the biggest aircraft manufacturer in the country – Vickers were producing their own designs and manufacturing Farnborough designs under licence, while Sopwith, prolific in both design and manufacture, had acquired additional premises in Kingston.

The new Croydon Airport in 1921. Plough Lane ran through the centre and aircraft had to cross the road via a level crossing. (London Borough of Sutton Heritage Service)

14

The government had authorised the building of National Aircraft Factories. The first one was sited at Waddon, near Croydon, on the other side of Plough Lane and adjacent to the Home Defence aerodrome of Beddington, and opened in January 1918. It was short-lived, and when the war ended in November that year the dismantling of the RAF began. With such a rapid disbanding a great surplus of aircraft was inevitable – production at Vickers at Brooklands fell, and Sopwith at Kingston went into liquidation in 1920.

While the RAF struggled to survive in the post-war world, the government promoted civil aviation. The first ever transatlantic flight took place in a Brooklands-built Vickers Vimy, flown by Captain J. Alcock and Lieutenant A. Whitten-Brown, on the 14th-15th June 1919. The following year, on 29th March, the new Croydon aerodrome opened, formed by the merger of the Home Defence aerodrome at Beddington and that of the National Aircraft Factory (later Air Disposal Company) at Waddon. By 1926 work had begun on enlarging and modernising Croydon Airport and in 1928 the enlarged site covering 330 acres could accommodate the biggest aircraft of the day. It became the most modern airport in Europe with the first custom-built terminal block, and set the standard for other major airports to follow.

Fortunately, Kenley survived the dismantling of the service by operating communication flights and by 1923 was supporting one fighter squadron, No 32, with Sopwith Snipes. The gradual expansion revived the flagging aircraft industry. Sopwith were taken over by H. G. Hawker Engineering Co. Ltd and work began at Kingston, with test flying at Brooklands.

A milestone in Surrey aviation history came in 1930, when a small field between Gatwick racecourse and Lowfield Heath was acquired by a Mr R. Waters, and Mr J. Mockford who founded the Surrey Aero Club. The field, alongside the river Mole, suffered in winter from heavy flooding and they sold out to Redwing Aircraft, who also had plans for development. The London to Brighton railway line alongside the site was soon to be electrified, which meant London would be only thirty minutes away by fast train. The site continued to defeat its owners, however, and in 1934 Redwing sold out to Airports Ltd. This company successfully drained the airfield, and built hangars and their own railway station. On 6th June 1936 the new London (South) Airport was opened.

Civil aviation was booming. In its golden era, Croydon was the busiest airport in Europe and internationally recognised as the leader in air transport, with Gatwick soon a strong contender for an alternative London airport. Redhill had opened in 1934, with British Air Transport

Empire Air Day at Kenley in 1938 when 3 Squadron were newly equipped with Hurricane Is. A Hawker Demon can be seen taxiing in the background. (Flight)

moving from their field in Lodge Lane, Addington, and was established as a training airfield, while smaller fields had opened at Ditton Hill, Hook and Hamsey Green. Brooklands had recovered from post-war economic difficulties and was producing aircraft for the now expanding RAF.

Aviation was now caught up in the spiral to war. In 1937 the RAFVR was expanded to train pilots and aircrew for the new squadrons now being created. Elementary & Reserve Flying Training Schools were opened and operated by civilian companies at Redhill, Gatwick and the new aerodrome at Fairoaks near Chobham. In 1938 the Civil Air Guard Scheme was launched, and Redhill Flying Club and the Insurance Flying Club at Gatwick participated.

Once war was declared Kenley, then the only RAF station in the county, became the sector controlling airfield with Croydon and Gatwick impressed as satellites. Redhill and Fairoaks continued as Elementary Flying Training Schools and Brooklands became solely concerned with aircraft production. The Civil Air Guard ceased to exist and the airfields of Hook and Hamsey Green closed. The 'phoney war' which followed gave a breathing space for defences to be completed and as the war progressed new airfields came into existence as the situation demanded. RAF Dunsfold opened in December 1942 as an Army Co-operation airfield, Wisley as a grass airfield in 1943 to assist Brooklands in flight testing, and the Advanced Landing Ground at Horne in April 1944.

The Defences

The airfields had two forms of defence – the general afforded by an umbrella of anti-aircraft guns, balloons and fighters, and the specific afforded by the airfield itself, often by measures decided on site.

The general defence plan was much as had been laid down in 1917 when it first became apparent there was a vital need for the early detection and plotting of enemy raiders, and the efficient control of fighters and guns from the ground. Then, Brigadier General Ashmore had realised the need for sufficient observation posts, backed up by searchlights controlled by sound detectors. These would pass on information through sub-controls to a central control room directing gun belts on the coast and around London and other vital targets, with fighters operating between the gun belts. Balloon barrages were placed strategically around cities and vital targets.

The essential difference between the defences of 1917 and 1939 was the introduction and use of radar, the electronic all-seeing eye. Before, raiders were normally detected visually when they crossed the coast,

The radar Chain Home seaward facing towers, transmitter left and receiver right. (Imperial War Museum)

17

A heavy anti-aircraft gun battery in Richmond Park, with the command post containing the predictor and height-finding units on the right. (Imperial War Museum)

giving little time for fighters to take off, climb and intercept, but now radar could detect aircraft 100 miles away and fighters could be scrambled or patrols vectored in good time to meet the attack, sometimes even before reaching the coast of England. Information from the seaward-facing chain of radar stations on the coast and sightings from the many Royal Observer Corps posts could be fed via their collection centres to the filter room of Fighter Command and to the sector-controlling airfields.

Searchlights, in groups of two or three, were spaced every few miles with a sound locator and a Lewis gun for protection, initially the 90 cm type but later 120 cm in diameter and radar-controlled. The heavy AA gun belts in the south were around London and the coastal ports, and in Surrey around the Brooklands and Bramley areas. The 3.7 inch and 4.5 inch guns were controlled by predictor gear and later by radar.

18

Croydon 1942. Part of a mixed AA gun battery, with ATS girls operating the height finder. (Mrs A. Viebahn)

The first 'local' line of airfield defence was a passive one – deception. The whole site, including the buildings and in some cases the ground itself, was camouflaged by painting simulated hedges, footpaths etc on the grass or concrete. Large buildings were draped with rope netting. Sometimes a complete decoy airfield was constructed with dummy buildings, aircraft and lorries and even simulated lighting effects. Gatwick had such a site at Lower Beeding. Access to airfields was restricted and in some cases roads nearby were closed or re-routed (as at Hayes Lane, Kenley) with signposts removed. Blast protection to buildings was accomplished with walls of sandbags. Barbed wire abounded, slit trenches were dug and air raid shelters built. Aircraft were dispersed around the field in E-shaped blast pens, 150 to 190 feet wide and 80 feet deep. Two machines could shelter here, with an air raid shelter in the rear wall for the ground crews.

Active local defence meant that most airfields had a couple of three-inch anti-aircraft guns, many of First World War vintage. They were effective only up to about 14,500 feet but had the advantage of more rapid fire (15 rounds a minute) than the heavier ones. However, the most effective against low-flying attacks was undoubtedly the 40 mm Bofors rapid-firing AA gun at 120 rounds a minute. These would be supplemented by the lighter 20 mm Hispano cannon and machine

A Type 24 pill box, which was situated at strategic defence points, still stands on the approach road to Redhill and Horne. (Author)

guns, the latter mounted at strategic positions, often in or on top of brick-built pill boxes. These boxes also guarded access roads around the site and many can still be seen today.

The novel and secret parachute and cable AA weapon was not tried until the raids on the Battle of Britain airfields. Batteries of rocket launchers were sited in the expected path of low-flying aircraft to fire salvoes of rockets up to 600 feet, each rocket trailing a steel cable. When they reached the specified height, two parachutes would open suspending a 480 foot steel cable between them which would wrap around the wing of any aircraft flying into it. When first used during the Kenley raid, one aircraft was brought down.

Although the main threat to an airfield was obviously from aerial attack by enemy bombers, as the war progressed it seemed that land-based attack might also be a possibility and many defence exercises were mounted against this eventuality. Ground defences were augmented by army and later RAF Regiment troops, and squadron personnel were issued with sidearms. At times, due to shortage of equipment, it was left to individual airfields to 'make do and mend' and many innovative ideas for defence emerged. They included mobile pill boxes and armour-plated lorries with machine guns. The latter,

20

'Make do and mend' defences included the Armadillo armoured vehicle, a converted lorry that could house a gunner in the pill box. (R. G. Moss)

called Armadillos, were designed to move swiftly down runways in the event of paratroop or airborne landings.

In the later stages of the war, when the V1 menace began, most airfields in the firing line were just ticking over, their squadrons having moved to France with the invasion forces. No local defence was effective against these new weapons and so the sites were closed and became balloon centres, operating barrage balloons as part of the defence curtain spread across from Cobham in Kent to Limpsfield and later Redhill in Surrey.

Airfield Buildings and Design

The first airfields were of necessity simply flat, well-drained grass areas with no obstructions, to allow the flimsy early flying machines to take off and land in any direction into wind, and with a shed to house the aeroplane during adverse weather. As the number of machines grew, the first purpose-designed shed evolved as a wooden gable-ended building about 60 feet wide with sliding doors, in terraces of about twelve units like those built at Brooklands around 1910.

With the outbreak of war in 1914 the newly formed RFC sought new airfields and with the acquisition of farmland at Beddington temporary canvas Bessoneaux hangars were erected to get the Home Defence aerodrome operating as quickly as possible. Approximately 60 feet wide and 75 feet deep, they housed one aeroplane. All that was now needed was a shed with a telephone, and storage for rockets for signalling. Accommodation was under canvas.

The first Air Acceptance Park to be built was at Kenley, equipped with Bessoneaux hangars whilst permanent ones were built. From the start there was standardisation. Each shed was brick-built as a pair (sometimes three), the two bays each having a separate bow-string style roof, supported internally by wooden lattice Belfast-type beams supported on central columns and outside walls. Sliding doors were fitted, the overall width of 160 feet giving clear door openings to each bay of approximately half a span. Seven shed pairs were built at Kenley, three at Brooklands and one pair and one single at Beddington. Service aerodromes were instantly recognised and dominated by these buildings. The tented accommodation was replaced by single-storey barrack huts, ablutions and cookhouses whilst the technical site

The old wartime control tower at Redhill, demolished in January 1987. (Author)

contained a station HQ, motor transport section, sick quarters and a watch office to control the movements of aircraft. Initially this was just a shed but later some airfields had an office supported high on the side of a hangar, overlooking the flying ground, marked with a letter 'C'. On the ground in front of the watch office was the signal square for visual messages to aircraft regarding take off and landing direction, circuit pattern, prohibitions etc. A white chalk ring was situated in the centre of the landing ground with the aerodrome name cut into the chalk.

Later the importance of movement control for aircraft on the ground and in the air was realised and now that most aircraft had radio, purpose-built control towers were added. Normally of two storeys and brick-built, the top floor had all-round glass to give a 360° view of the airfield. Although equipped with radio and later with more advanced equipment such as radar, the visual signal square still remained. On some airfields the control tower was supplemented by a small caravan situated near to the end of the active runway controlling streams of take-offs by signal lamp.

With the end of the war the rapid growth of civil aviation offered a great challenge to architects and engineers to provide functional yet pleasing designs for the coming airports. The conditions for these airports would be vastly different from service operations. They would operate 365 days a year, with night flying depending on the weather, handling large numbers of people, freight and mail and subject to Customs for overseas flights.

The first post-war aerodrome was at Croydon, utilising the existing buildings of the old Beddington and Waddon aerodromes. Expansion was rapid and in six years this makeshift airport was to be enlarged and modernised. In 1928 the new airport emerged as the most modern in Europe. Thought had been given to the flow of passengers by co-ordinating road transport with air travel. Passengers would arrive by car or coach at the entrance of the custom-built terminal block, with a walk through a hall containing the airline counters, Customs and Immigration controls and then on through the exit to waiting airliners. Positioned over the exit was a large control tower 50 feet high overseeing the airfield and housing the latest in wireless communications, direction finding and blind flying equipment, together with a meteorological office. It was ideal for civil flying, but not as a war station as it was destined to become in such a short time.

In 1931 Kenley was modernised to house two permanent fighter squadrons. There was sufficient hangarage but the domestic and

The officers' mess at Kenley was a fine example of RAF architecture used in the 1930s expansion era. (P. Flint)

technical buildings needed uprating. Kenley was one of the first to benefit from the early expansion schemes. The resultant building improvements based on Air Ministry designs had to receive approval from the Royal Fine Arts Commission, and had to be both functional and pleasing. They eventually formed the basis of future developments. Gone were the austere single-storey barrack huts, to be replaced by modern brick-built, two-storey buildings equipped with all the modern conveniences. The main buildings, station HQ, main gate, guard room, officers' mess etc were brick and tile-built to an adopted mock-Georgian style, the result being some fine buildings, many of which are preserved and in use today.

The technical site was improved and petrol storage increased to 30,000 gallons, while the armoury was allowed to hold 500,000 rounds of ammunition. An operations building was introduced equipped with radio and direct telephone and teleprinter lines to control.

1935 saw the expansion programme accelerate. The Air Ministry Works Directorate was formed to oversee the design and progress of new airfields. Hangars were one of the first aspects to receive consideration. The original 1917 Belfast design had door openings

24

which were too small for the new generation of aircraft, with their much bigger wingspans. The early designs, type A, were based on the Belfast principle but made of steel framing covered in corrugated iron and having a 120 foot span. Type C was steel-framed with brick infill, having a new style roof consisting of twelve small gable sections like saw teeth, and a span of 150 feet.

The approach of the war brought an urgent need for additional hangars and the prefabricated transportable designs arrived on the scene. The Bellman of 95 foot span and the T types were all gable-ended, steel-framed and covered with corrugated iron. RAF Dunsfold, built in 1942, has two T2-type hangars still standing.

By far the most common and widely used temporary hangar from 1941 onwards was the Blister type manufactured by Miskins. It consisted of a curved section of corrugated iron incorporating walls and roof, either 60 feet or 69 feet wide by 25 feet deep, capable of housing one small aircraft and used by ground crews as a shelter whilst carrying out servicing. A larger Dorman Long type, 90 feet wide, was introduced in 1943. The open ends could be fitted with curtains but many had the openings bricked up and are still in use. For accommodation, workshops or offices, many small prefabricated buildings were used such as the Maycrete, constructed of precast concrete slabs and posts, and the famous Nissen hut, a design from the First World War, that sprang up in profusion. Of semi-circular section, it consisted of corrugated iron, sometimes lined, in spans of 16 to 30 feet with the ends filled in with wood, and a stove for heating. It was known to every serviceman.

Buildings were important but an airfield could not operate without its landing areas. Originally grass, they were subject to the weather, some becoming wet and muddy and non-operational, but with the new generation of fighters and bombers demanding longer take-off runs and greater load-bearing surfaces, hard runways were introduced, connected to the hardstanding by perimeter tracks. Some existing airfields were closed whilst hard runways were laid. Kenley closed in September 1939 for six months to enlarge the airfield and lay two concrete runways 1,000 yards long, extended later to 1,200 yards to enable Hurricanes and Spitfires to operate safely. New airfields would have reinforced concrete runways laid from the start, sometimes coated with bitumen and often laid in a triangular pattern. In all cases the main runway was longer than the other two and facing into the prevailing wind. In 1939 the minimum requirements for runways were 1,000 yards for fighters and 2,000 yards by 50 yards for airfields operating bombers. Dunsfold, built in 1942, operated both. Grass airfields which had to be quickly pressed into service were improved by the laying of steel mesh tracking of various kinds on the runways.

Fighter Command

Formed in 1936 with the break up of the old Air Defence of Great Britain into its respective command functions, and headed by Air Marshal Sir Hugh Dowding, the new headquarters of Fighter Command were sited at Bentley Priory, a rambling old country mansion at Stanmore, Middlesex.

Taking up command on 14th June 1936, Dowding had the task of building the still under-strength fighter force into a front line defence organisation. On arrival he had nine fighter airfields holding 14 home-based squadrons equipped with biplane fighters like Gloster Gauntlets and Gladiators, Hawker Demons and Furies. He decided with the limited resources at his command to initially form two groups, geographically opposing the potential main threat – No 11 Group in the south of England, and No 12 Group in the east. These were subdivided into sectors, each controlled by a master airfield, having its own control or operations room linked to the main control at Bentley Priory. The only pre-war fighter station in Surrey was Kenley and this took over the role of controlling airfield for Sector B.

By September 1938 the number of fighter squadrons had risen to 30 and now included four Hurricane squadrons (Nos 87, 56, 73 and 111) with more in the process of converting to Hurricanes and Spitfires. As more squadrons became available new groups were formed to defend the rest of the country. The army was also expanding and Dowding worked closely with the newly formed AA Command under General Sir Frederick Pile, a liaison which would be needed in the conflict to come.

When war started, Fighter Command was stronger than envisaged with 42 squadrons of Hurricanes and Spitfires, six of Blenheim IFs, and two of Defiants. By the time of the Battle of Britain, Fighter Command had about 600 to 700 fighter aircraft, whilst the Luftwaffe with its three Airfleets in Norway, Holland and France could raise with advantage about 980 fighters.

As the tide of war turned and plans for the invasion of Europe were drawn up, it was felt that a special air force was required to move with the invasion fleet and the armies. It had to be similar to the 1st Tactical Air Force so successfully used in the Desert and North African landings. Named the 2nd Tactical Air Force, it comprised four Groups – Nos 83 and 84 strike squadrons of Spitfires and Typhoons, No 85 for defence of the army and air force, and No 2 of light bombers drawn from Bomber Command. By 1943 Fighter Command had lost two thirds of its squadrons to the 2nd TAF and reverted for a time (until October 1944) to its old title of Air Defence of Great Britain.

Balloon Command

Balloon Command was formed in 1938 to operate the balloon barrage around cities and vital targets which was used as a deterrent to low flying aircraft and dive bombing. The barrage in Surrey was controlled by No 2 Balloon Centre at Hook with about 135 balloons flown to the north of Brooklands. Each balloon was 62 feet long and 25 feet across, hydrogen filled and controlled by a cable and winch. They flew normally at 1,000 to 5,000 feet. However, it was not until 1944 with the

A barrage balloon in a typical Surrey setting. (Croydon Local Studies Library)

low flying V1 attacks that the balloon came into its own. The Surrey balloons formed part of a curtain from Cobham in Kent to Redhill in Surrey, the last defence before London, with the airfield at Redhill becoming No 24 Balloon Centre. By the time the threat was over the balloons had accounted for 211 'divers'.

Training and Reserve Commands

Training Command was formed along with the other commands in 1936. Reserve Command was formed in 1939 to look after the new voluntary reserve centres and the civilian-run elementary flying training schools.

Training facilities had operated for Auxiliary Air Force and reserve pilots to keep their hand in, but in 1936 the government proposed the expansion of the voluntary reserve with the Direct Entry Scheme and new centres with civilian-operated Elementary & Reserve Flying Training Schools were opened at Redhill, Gatwick, Fairoaks, and for a short while at Kenley. To qualify, direct entrants had to be 18 to 25 years old, medically fit, and educated to School Certificate standard. They would join for five years, being sworn in as sergeant pilots, and receive 12s 6d per day when trained. In consequence, the flying clubs began to suffer financially and the government, realising the importance of civilian flying training, introduced the Civil Air Guard scheme, administered by honorary civilian commissioners, whereby successful men and women applicants aged 18 to 50 and medically fit would receive subsidised flying training at a club, to A licence standard. This could cost them as little as 2s 6d per hour instead of the usual £2 to £3, the only stipulation being that they should give an honorary undertaking to give their services to any branch of the armed services if required.

When war started the CAG, which operated a scheme at Redhill Flying Club and the Insurance Flying Club at Gatwick, ceased to function and the reserve schools became Elementary Flying Training Schools.

The Final Rehearsal

Each year Air Defence Exercises were held to test the efficiency of the combined air and ground defences against an attack and the one in 1939 held a special significance. From 8th to 11th August 1939, 1,300 machines took part in the greatest ever exercise in conjunction with the AA, balloons, Royal Observer Corps and the new radar, and for the first time the Air Raid Precaution personnel and a trial blackout were included.

In the exercise 500 fighters – Spitfires, Hurricanes, Blenheims and Gladiators – of the defending 'Westland' force from 26 aerodromes (Kenley was temporarily inactive due to improvement work) defended an area in the South East against an 'Eastland' enemy bomber force of Wellingtons, Battles and Hampdens, coming from somewhere in the North Sea. Attacks were made day and night against targets in the south, Isle of Wight and London, the accuracy of the bombing calculated by the bombers flashing Sashalite lamps simulating bomb release to be caught by hidden cameras on the ground. At the end of the exercise the official opinion was that the fighter defence was a match for any raiding bomber, and a 'Well done, everybody' was signalled to all stations from Sir Hugh Dowding.

The final rehearsal was over. The scene was set. War commenced on 3rd September 1939.

2
DUNSFOLD

In 1941 the commander of the 1st Canadian Army, Lt General A. G. L. McNaughton, whose army had been training in Britain for over a year, became concerned that only two RCAF Army Co-operation squadrons had been formed instead of the originally proposed six. In addition, no airfields had been made available for them to use, despite an agreement with Sir Charles Portal, Chief of Air Staff. At a further meeting with Air Ministry officials in 1942, General McNaughton was told that due to the heavy workload of airfield expansion they could not guarantee an airfield for at least another 18 months. Undaunted, he declared that he would construct his own airfields using Royal Canadian Army engineers if he was provided with the land and building materials. This was agreed and the energetic General took over a piece of rich pastureland set in the beautiful wooded area to the east of Dunsfold village and two and a half miles south of Cranleigh.

General McNaughton and Major General Hertzberg, Chief Engineer of the Canadian Army, met with Sir Charles Portal on 22nd April 1942 to request permission to commence construction. They set themselves a target of 18 weeks to completion. The reputation of the Royal Canadian Army Engineers was on the line, and almost before the ink on the agreement was dry, work had begun.

It was originally envisaged as a fighter airfield but was built to Air Ministry A-class bomber airfield standards with three hard runways and widely dispersed buildings and hardstandings. Work commenced officially on 11th May 1942 under the site direction of Major H. D. Duff MC. Using massive American earth-moving equipment, work progressed at a cracking pace. Acres of Surrey countryside were sacrificed to the needs of war and Robbins Farm and Hall Place cottages had to be demolished.

An impassioned plea from one lady owner to save her cottage, which would have been on the runway, was answered by an innovative Canadian crew led by sergeants Kreuger and Whidden. They dug out

The first Mustang to visit the new airfield, on 17th August 1942, flown by Flight Lieutenant Bissky of 400 Squadron.

completely beneath the building, sliding in beech logs as they went, and the complete cottage was then towed on the sledge of logs by three large tractors to a new resting place half a mile away. There it remained for many years, used first as a squadron office and later as a dwelling.

On 3rd June General McNaughton was able to conduct important visitors around the rapidly evolving site and on the 20th the first aircraft arrived, a Tiger Moth from 414 Squadron RCAF based at Croydon which landed on a strip of recently completed perimeter track. By the 15th the runways and perimeter track were complete but the stark white concrete glaring in the sun had to be camouflaged by spraying with a mixture of tar and wood chippings. On the 17th the first Mustang arrived, piloted by Flight Lieutenant Paul Bissky from

400 Squadron RCAF at Odiham.

On 16th October 1942 the site was officially handed over to Air Marshal Edwards, RCAF. The ceremony included the unveiling of a commemorative plinth sculpted by a Royal Canadian Engineer, Sapper Trenka, and ended with a flypast of a mixed formation of 400 and 414 Squadron Mustangs who then completed a landing on the new aerodrome.

The three runways were now finished, along with 49 hardstandings, but the two T2 hangars, eleven Blisters, technical and domestic sites were not ready until the end of the year. In early December No 2 site was occupied by the station HQ and No 39 Army Co-operation Wing RCAF moved in. On the 5th, 414 (AC) Squadron commanded by Wing Commander Begg, with their Mustang Is, arrived from Croydon to what was a very wet and muddy site, followed by a small detachment of Mustangs from 400 (AC) Squadron who occupied No 1 site.

By the end of December the technical site was almost complete and, weather permitting, flying training commenced, using Tangmere as an alternate aerodrome. The training consisted of exercises with the Canadian army who were stationed nearby and in other parts of the

A fine example of a Blister hangar, 1943, with a Mustang of 400 Squadron undergoing checks. (National Archives of Canada)

32

south of England. On 21st December ground-to-air communications were practised with armoured cars and troop carriers on Ludshott Common, as a demonstration for *Movietone News*.

As 1943 dawned many airmen were on leave but those remaining in camp celebrated the new year with a special dinner. It also heralded the formation of a new squadron, No 430 (AC) at Hartfordbridge, which flew into Dunsfold on the following day with 14 Tomahawks, split into two flights. Wing Commander E. Moncrief AFC took over as temporary station commander.

While 400 Squadron moved out to Middle Wallop for a month during January, 414 Squadron carried out several practice shoots at Weston Zoyland. At Dunsfold a blanket of snow covered the airfield in the early part of January, followed by rain which turned the airfield to mud. Wellington boots were the order of the day! By the end of the month, however, the airfield was firmly established and Wing Commander J. H. Burden took over as permanent officer in command, whilst the weather improved and local flying commenced.

At the beginning of February 414 moved out for a spell at Middle Wallop, while 400 returned with 19 aircraft. By 8th February, 430 Squadron had changed completely to Mustangs and these three squadrons were to be the main complement of Army Co-operation, later redesignated Fighter Reconnaissance, aircraft based at Dunsfold. During the month 400 Squadron had a spell at Weston Zoyland and on the 25th celebrated its third anniversary of landing in England. No 430 carried out a dummy attack on Kenley aerodrome, together with photo-shoots, and on the 21st, 414 returned from Middle Wallop.

All three squadrons now commenced training for the army exercise codenamed Spartan, which was scheduled for the coming month. Over 1,200 personnel gathered for the exercise, which occupied the first two weeks of March. It was designed to test the ability of squadrons to move quickly from site to site whilst engaged in ground attack on enemy troops and equipment. The airfield itself took no part in the exercise, the men moving out and operating from temporary bases. Living under canvas was seen as a rehearsal for things to come.

On 26th March, 414 flew its first successful 'Rhubarb' operation. Two Mustangs flown by Flying Officers Stover and Hutchinson attacked and destroyed an electrical transformer and two locomotives. The Rhubarb operations (attacks on targets of opportunity) were highly dangerous, often flown in bad weather and low cloud. This was demonstrated on the 27th when Flying Officers Stevens and Mossing took off from Dunsfold in misty conditions. On reaching the South

Coast they ran into dense fog. Ordered to return to base, Mossing climbed to 6,000 feet and obtained a 'homer' from Tangmere but Stevens tragically crashed his Mustang into the side of a hill to the north of Brighton.

By the end of March 1943 the number of aircraft in 400 Squadron had increased to 21 Mustangs, two Tomahawks, one Typhoon, one Magister and one Tiger Moth. Between 9th and 11th April, their first Rhubarb operations accounted for 19 locomotives destroyed, while 13 photographic sorties over France collected information for invasion planners. At night, Ranger operations were carried out: on the 13th, Flying Officer Grant joined in the circuit of a bomber night-flying school at the Melun Villarouche airfield to the south of Paris and shot down a Dornier 217. On the 26th more Ranger operations took place in the St Valery area. Unfortunately the aircraft were picked up by searchlights, with one Mustang being hit whilst the pilot, Flying Officer Pepper, baled out. These sorties continued to the end of April.

Dunsfold, with its all-weather facilities and Darky homing beacon, became an ideal emergency airfield and on 4th April, a Fortress landed short of fuel and with wounded on board. On the night of the 11th, two Wellingtons were successfully guided in.

On 1st April, two Mustangs flew a Rhubarb to St Pierre but one was hit by flak and the aircraft was lost. More flying training was carried out, with low level navigation instruction, photographic sorties etc, until 9th April when 400 Squadron moved to Middle Wallop.

Meanwhile, 430 Squadron were still working up to operational standard. On 26th May they flew their first operational Rhubarb against railways in the Lisieux and Alençon areas. On the 28th, until bad weather intervened, they attacked railways in the areas of Mézidon to Argentan and Amiens, Poix and Neufchatel. That month a Whitley towing a Horsa glider arrived to transport a detachment of 430 Squadron personnel on an army co-operation exercise. Meanwhile, 2847 AA Squadron arrived, together with No 403 Repair and Salvage Unit.

On 1st June 1943 the Army Co-operation Command was broken up and RCAF Dunsfold was transferred to No 11 Group, Fighter Command with the squadrons redesignated as Fighter Reconnaissance. At this time the intricate planning for the invasion of Europe was well in hand. One requirement was the provision of suitable landing grounds which could be rapidly set up following the advance of the armies. In June an experimental runway laid at Dunsfold by the Royal Canadian Engineers proved a great success. Consisting of two-ply bonded hessian similar to heavy roofing felt, it measured 1,200 yards by 50 yards and was laid on ground which had been graded and compacted, then rolled. On the 23rd, VIPs watched as four Spitfires from Redhill made repeated landings on the strip, followed by four Dunsfold Mustangs, then a Mosquito and a Wellington. Finally, a Marauder with a tricycle undercarriage landed to show the all-round capability of the runway.

Dominion Day on 1st July was celebrated with a Rhubarb attack by two Mustangs from 414. It also saw the Dunsfold Fighter Reconnaissance squadrons incorporated into the 2nd Tactical Air Force and the formation of mobile airfields. On 5th July, parts of 414 and 430 Squadrons moved to Gatwick to form No 129 Airfield.

The next two days saw the arrival of 231 Squadron with Mustangs and on the 13th, No 128 Airfield was formed from 400 Squadron and the remainder of 414 and 430 Squadrons. With the formation of the mobile airfields, the role of Dunsfold was changing. On the 19th it was announced that it was to be administered by Kenley and would be put on a care and maintenance basis. 231 Squadron was disbanded and on the 26th, No 128 Airfield moved out to the new Advanced Landing Ground at Woodchurch. Dunsfold was closed temporarily due to lack of signals and control staff but some aircraft under repair with No 403 Repair and Service Unit remained.

In early August the airfield was inspected with a view to No 2 Group, 2nd Tactical Air Force taking it over and operating bombers. On the 12th an advance party arrived and the next day Dunsfold was reopened as aircraft started to arrive – two Halifaxes and a Lancaster returned from a raid on Milan, whilst another Lancaster unfortunately crashed three miles from the airfield. Further aircraft arrived in the form of a Stirling and three Halifaxes after a raid in Italy.

The 16th saw the arrival of 700 personnel of 98 and 180 Squadrons and the reopening of the officers' quarters at Hall Place and Stovoldshill Farm. The aircrews of 180 Squadron soon replaced those of 414 at The Three Compasses pub, while the ground crews preferred the Leathern Bottle on the Guildford Road.

By 20th August the Royal Canadian Army Service Corps had unloaded a large shipment of 500 lb and 1,000 lb bombs from Witley station and transported them to the airfield, where the normal storage was for 200 tons. No 228 Maintenance Unit moved into the camp site at Sachel Court. The next day the Mitchell bombers of the new squadrons, 98 and 180, arrived.

The North American B25 Mitchell was a medium day-bomber

NA B25 Mitchell II of 98 Squadron, 2nd TAF, painted with invasion identification stripes. (MAP)

powered by two Wright Cyclone 1,700 hp or 1,850 hp engines giving a top speed of 275 mph at 24,000 feet with a bomb load of 4,000 lbs. The aircraft, however, usually operated at 11,000 to 15,000 feet for accuracy of bombing, and in 'boxes' of six. The low operating altitude made them vulnerable to the highly effective fire of the 88 mm anti-aircraft guns.

At 7.30 am on 23rd August, 98 and 180 Squadrons each put up a box of six aircraft and bombed the railway marshalling yards at St Omer, all aircraft returning safely. On the 27th the aerodrome at Bernay St Martin was the target but heavy cloud cover made it impossible for the fighter escort to operate so the mission was cancelled and the aircraft returned still bombed-up. These bombing missions were in support of Operation Starkey, a feint attack in the Pas de Calais area to divert enemy forces from other situations and draw their fighters into the air to be dealt with by the escorting Spitfires. The ploy did not achieve great success as only a limited number of fighters rose to the bait, while the Mitchells were subjected to murderous ack-ack fire.

The Dunsfold squadrons often flew with other Mitchell and Boston squadrons such as 226 from Hartfordbridge, the Mitchells frequently leading the way in bad weather as they were equipped with the GEE navigation system.

On 30th August, twelve aircraft from 98 Squadron and twelve from 180 Squadron attacked oil dumps in the Forest of Eperlecques where it was thought V1 launching sites were being constructed. Here 180 suffered its first loss, a Mitchell hit by flak. As the aircraft went down three parachutes were seen to open.

The attacks were stepped up in September over the forests of Hesdin and Eperlecques, and twelve aircraft set out for the Monch-Breton airfield but returned bombed-up as cloud obscured the target. On the 4th there were two sorties of 18 Mitchells from 98 and 180 Squadrons. The railway marshalling yards at Rouen and Sotteville were attacked in the morning, the aircraft then returning to be rearmed, and in the afternoon the heavily fortified E-boat pens in the Bassin Lambert in the Boulogne docks were bombed. No enemy aircraft were encountered but the flak was very heavy. One hundred tons of bombs were dropped during the day. Two days later the attack on the E-boat pens was repeated, when a large orange flash was seen coming from the target. With again very heavy flak, one Mitchell was hit and crash-landed at Dungeness with no loss of life.

The 7th brought attacks on the St Omer marshalling yards, and also confirmation that Dunsfold was now part of No 2 Group, 2nd Tactical Air Force. The next day saw two missions, attacking Vitry-en-Artois aerodrome and Fort de la Creche.

No 320 Royal Dutch Naval Air Service Squadron from Lasham, with 14 Mitchells and 28 crews, now temporarily joined 98 and 180 to operate from Dunsfold. The next day, 9th September, as dawn broke 36 Mitchells from the three squadrons roared off the Dunsfold runway to attack gun positions in the Boulogne area and in the afternoon 18 aircraft bombed the Monch-Breton airfield. This combined operation signalled the end of Operation Starkey and on the following day 320 Squadron returned to Lasham.

On the airfield there were few recreational facilities for the personnel but the commanding officer, Wing Commander Burden was pleased at this time to be able to open a camp cinema which it was hoped would make the long blackout nights more bearable.

On 21st September, 18 aircraft of 98 and 180 Squadrons attacked the synthetic petrol plant at Lens from 12,000 feet. One Mitchell was hit by cannon fire from a Fw 190 over Hesdin, dived and exploded on the ground. Another, also hit by cannon fire over Hesdin from a Fw 190 which had broken through the escorting screen of Spitfires, ditched in the sea near Berck sur Mer with Flight Sergeant Davis and his crew being picked up later by an Air-Sea Rescue launch. Up to the end of

*Dunsfold 1943. Bombing up and refuelling a NA B25 Mitchell II of 180 Squadron.
(Imperial War Museum)*

September these Ramrod operations continued, including raids on
Brest aerodrome and the Amiens marshalling yards.

Returning aircraft from other squadrons continued to use Dunsfold
in emergencies. On 2nd October 1943, two Halifaxes landed at night,
one aircraft accidentally dropping a 1,000 lb bomb on the perimeter
track whilst taxiing! Fortunately it did not explode and was safely
defused by the station armament officer.

October saw a start to night flying training, which was not very
popular with the daylight bombing crews, and later that month the
villagers of Cranleigh were alarmed when the local railway station was
evacuated and the village cordoned off for the arrival of a special
military train. RAF personnel donned anti-gas capes and clothing, and
the local fire brigade stood by whilst a deadly cargo was unloaded and
transported to the aerodrome. On arrival the assembled personnel were
told that it was mustard gas. Although prohibited under international

agreement, if the enemy used this ghastly weapon in a last desperate situation, the men were told, then retaliation would be by precision bombing by the Mitchell squadrons. After a demonstration the weapons were returned to the main dump, to the relief of all concerned.

In November 1943, Fighter Command was disbanded and replaced by two structures, the Air Defence of Great Britain and the 2nd Tactical Air Force. Dunsfold was designated No 139 Airfield in No 2 Group, 2nd TAF under the group's commander, Air Vice Marshal Sir Basil Embry. A new pattern of bombing raids was now established. It was known that a great number of construction sites existed in northern France for V1 launching (Noball) sites and these were to be pounded constantly. On 5th November the Crossbow operations commenced with twelve Mitchells each from 98 and 180 Squadrons joining with 24 other Mitchells and 24 Bostons, escorted by 18 squadrons of Spitfires, to attack a huge site at Mimoyecques, south-west of Calais. Bad weather forced the Bostons to return but the Mitchells continued on to bomb the target using their GEE navigation. These sites were heavily defended and the flak made accurate bombing difficult. The target was raided again on the 8th and once again the flak was a great problem. A few days later the village of Audinghen, the headquarters of the construction site at Mimoyecqes, was attacked.

On 11th November there was a change of command as Wing Commander Burden relinquished his post and was replaced by another Canadian, Group Captain L. Dunlap RCAF. Bad weather was now hampering operations but on the 25th it cleared and Dunlap accompanied one of the crews of 180 Squadron on a raid to attack a V1 manufacturing site at Martinvast. On the bombing run three aircraft from the box in which he was flying were suddenly blown out of the sky by a fierce concentration of ack-ack fire. Luckily, the three remaining aircraft survived but it was a salutary reminder of the dangers of daylight bombing and on return Dunlap immediately arranged a concentrated programme of night flying. He and Air Vice Marshal Embry often flew with crews on the night-flying exercises to give them encouragement for the 'round the clock' operations to come.

Bad weather once again restricted operations but just before Christmas 1943 some old friends in the form of B flight of 400 Squadron arrived from Redhill with their Mosquito PR XVIs. The squadron's role had changed from fighter-reconnaissance to purely photo-reconnaissance and they had given up their Mustangs. Redhill was unsuitable for operating the Mosquito on the conversion course,

Pilots of 400 (City of Toronto) Squadron at Dunsfold, 26th November 1943, with NA Mustang I. (National Archives of Canada)

but was satisfactory for A flight which had switched to Spitfire XIs.

In the new year further Crossbow raids were carried out on Noball sites. On 4th February 1944, B flight of 400 Squadron left with their Mosquitos for Odiham, making room for the return of the 'Flying Dutchmen'. On the 10th, 320 Squadron RDNAS arrived with their Mitchells and ground crew to take up permanent residence alongside 98 and 180 Squadrons, their dark blue naval uniforms contrasting sharply with the familiar RAF blue.

They were soon in action on 12th February with 98 and 180, and on the 24th they teamed up with 226 Squadron from Hartfordbridge to attack a Noball target at St Josef, where once again the flak was particularly heavy. Twenty three aircraft led by Wing Commander Lynn successfully bombed the target from 8,000 feet in clear skies.

One aircraft captained by Jan Maas was caught in the vicious flak, shrapnel peppering the fuselage and severing the hydraulic systems.

Photo technicians removing an aerial camera from a Mustang of 430 Squadron, March 1944. (National Archives of Canada)

Another hit tore a hole in the floor and roof and the port engine began to labour. Reporting the damage to his leader, Maas's aircraft left the formation. His young navigator, on his first mission, joined Maas in the cockpit and they were soon crossing the French coast home. Realising, with the damage sustained, he would not make Dunsfold, Maas was directed to the small grass airfield of Friston, the first on the route into England, situated high on the white cliffs just west of Beachy Head. At 4,000 feet, losing height and with 15 miles to run, it was touch and go. Finally, with the port engine about to pack up and the starboard whining with overwork, Friston was located below in the mist by the navigator, its two naturally formed runways amongst the snow-covered, undulating farmland of Gayles Farm, pointing out to sea. Given a straight-in approach, Maas put the damaged aircraft down on the short grass runway, braking hard, and slithered to a stop only a short distance from some buildings at the end. Such occurrences were by now commonplace, some aircraft making it to land, others falling victims of the Channel.

On the same day Maas made it home, 18 aircraft from 98 and 180 Squadrons, escorted by Typhoons, attacked the Noball site in the Bois d'Cocquerel. Large fires were started and the smoke could be seen all the way to the coast. Further attacks on Noball sites continued until March when the raids switched to railways, aerodromes and other targets.

In March night flying once again came to the fore. The squadrons participated in Exercise Nite-Lite, to find the best method of attacking convoys at night, either by the Mitchells themselves bombing, or by them dropping flares to illuminate the ground for Mosquitos to attack. At the end of the month each squadron in rotation went for a training session at Swanton Morley for formation flying at night. This was very unpopular and proved hazardous, 180 Squadron losing three aircraft. To test the effectiveness of Mitchells operating at night, a limited number of night attacks were made on Noball targets, the Mitchells bombing on flares dropped by Mosquitos.

On 18th April 1944, the Allied Supreme Commander, General Dwight Eisenhower arrived at Dunsfold in a Dakota from Hartford-bridge, accompanied by Air Chief Marshal Sir Trafford Leigh-Mallory, Air Marshal Sir Arthur Coningham, Air Vice Marshal Embry and Group Captain Atcherly, plus various other high ranking officers from the USAAF and US Army. After 98 and 320 Squadrons had been inspected (180 was away at Swanton Morley), General Eisenhower spoke to the assembled personnel about the importance of training and being prepared for the task ahead.

On 15th May it was announced that RAF Dunsfold would be transferred to 11 Group Air Defence of Great Britain, and that No 139 Airfield was to be renamed No 139 Wing of the 2nd Tactical Air Force. In preparation for its forthcoming mobile role it would remain on the airfield as a lodger, with only a holding party at Dunsfold itself. The airfield's personnel had already gone under canvas in preparation.

By the end of May, No 139 Wing's attacks on enemy airfields had increased in frequency as the invasion drew near, and the Wing now switched to night attacks. On 2nd June a night attack was made on the airfield at Beamont-le-Roger using GEE navigation equipment, each aircraft dropping eight 500 lb bombs from 12,000 feet, and on the 3rd a gun position at Fécamp was attacked. That day Operations Order No 3 arrived, outlining the part the Dunsfold Mitchell squadrons would play in the invasion – but when was it to come?

On an overcast 5th June 1944, all leave was stopped and personnel were restricted to camp. All telephone calls were stopped and it was thought by the men an exercise was in the offing. The aircraft had black and white identification stripes painted around the fuselage and wings and the squadrons were brought to readiness, the crews full of expectancy.

At 23 minutes past midnight on 6th June, twelve Mitchells of 320 Squadron took off, their target a bridge over the river Dives. One hour later twelve aircraft of 180 followed, their target a rail crossing at Argentan, and at 2.16 am 98 was the final squadron airborne with eleven aircraft detailed to bomb a railway line in a defile south of Thury Harcourt near Caen. The operation, however, did not run smoothly. The aircraft of 320 had problems with their GEE navigation systems equipment and as thick cloud made target identification impossible they returned to Dunsfold. Similar problems with the weather affected 180 and only eight aircraft found the target and bombed on target indicator flares laid by Mosquitos from Lasham; one aircraft found the secondary target and bombed the airfield at Argentan. Five of 98's aircraft bombed the defile at Thury Harcourt, again with the assistance of Lasham's Mosquitos, the remainder attacking the airfield at Conde-sur-Vire. At first light on the way home across the Channel, gaps in the cloud revealed to the bomber crews a great armada of ships below, escorted by hundreds of aircraft, steaming towards the French coast – the invasion had begun.

From now on No 139 Wing was employed on night operations, attacking targets as required by the advancing Allied army below. These could be extremely hazardous with so many aircraft brought together in the dark, heavily laden with fuel and bombs. On the night of 7th June 320 Squadron had taken off and were climbing out over Horsham when there was a blinding flash as two aircraft collided; one exploded immediately, the other a few minutes later.

On 10th June 1944, the Mitchells reverted to daylight attacks. An important tank concentration and the German Panzer headquarters had been identified in the village of La Caine, and the Wing had been held in readiness awaiting ideal weather conditions for an attack. When the time was right they joined 226 Squadron from Hartford-bridge to make up 71 Mitchells, escorted by 40 Typhoons. The Typhoons were to attack the tanks and vehicles from low level with rockets, followed by the Mitchells from 12,000 feet using the new G-H radar equipment. After the Typhoons had attacked, Wing Commander Lynn led the Mitchells in and through a gap in the clouds saw the bombs hit the target, the Chateau de la Caine, which erupted in flames and smoke. The attack was a great success, dealing a severe blow to the

German Panzer Group West.

The British GEE blind-navigation system was essentially a ground transmitter and a cathode ray tube receiver mounted in a box in the aircraft and displaying two bright green parallel lines running across the screen. Map co-ordinates of the destination were fed into it and two bright blips appeared on the screen. On the top line the blip moved across the screen until central, then a course was steered to keep the blip in place. When the second blip also reached centre point, the target had been reached. On the other hand, the new G-H system was essentially a small radar transmitter mounted in the aircraft, beaming to the ground. The bounced off rays traced out a picture of the ground below which was displayed on a receiver also mounted in the aircraft.

On the night of 11th June, 98 Squadron were the only aircraft to operate from Dunsfold and joined with Mosquitos from Gravesend and Hartfordbridge on Nite-Lite operations. The next day Queen Wilhelmina of the Netherlands, accompanied by Prince Bernhard, visited Dunsfold to speak to the Dutch squadron and present medals. They later watched as 320 took off with 98 Squadron to attack tank concentrations. The attack on the 21st Panzer Division servicing area was particularly successful.

On 13th June the first V1s were seen and an airfield construction unit arrived to be ready to deal with bomb craters. Dunsfold's defences were strengthened by the arrival of No 2879 RAF Regiment with two flights of Hispano cannon for use against the V1s. On 17th June the gunners had their first success, shooting down a V1 overhead, but their jubilation was short-lived when they were told to leave them alone in future in the hope they would pass harmlessly on.

Dunsfold was also home, temporarily, to 30 Mosquito Fb VIs of No 140 Wing, belonging to 464 Squadron RAAF, 487 Squadron RNZAF and 21 Squadron from Gravesend who felt that it was safer than their home airfield. They operated from here for a few nights before leaving for Thorney Island.

Despite the V1 activity operations still continued against Noball sites, but on 22nd June an urgent call came from the Army for some precision bombing. The German army had dug in around the Caen area, slowing the Allied advance. They had taken over the Colombelles steelworks on the eastern side of the Orne river and had the 51st Highland Division pinned down on the west side. There were only 1,000 yards separating the two forces, and the steelworks was heavily defended with 88 mm ack-ack guns, but 98 and 180's Mitchells and Bostons from Hartfordbridge attacked with pinpoint accuracy,

A V1 flying bomb or 'doodle bug', Hitler's Vergeltungswaffen (weapon of retaliation), in flight skimming the treetops. (D. Collyer)

completely destroying the works. No aircraft were lost and the Highlanders stormed across and dislodged the German troops.

As the summer wore on No 139 Wing was operating to capacity assisting the armies below as they advanced through France and the Low Countries. On 8th September 98 Squadron was detailed to attack the Boulogne guns, two boxes of six aircraft each being given separate targets. The Mitchells attacked the targets without loss but on the return it was noted that two aircraft were in trouble, with their bombs hung up.

One had the full cargo of eight bombs stuck and the other just one. Over the Channel both aircraft tried to jettison them but to no avail and the prospect of landing at Dunsfold was daunting. The crew with the single bomb had tried to hammer the release mechanism free but without success. At Dunsfold the aircraft with the full load landed safely but as the other aircraft touched down the bomb fell free and exploded, the flaming wreckage covering the runway. The whole crew were killed, as was a fitter who was standing in front of the hangars, hit in the chest by flying metal.

On 17th September the Wing was put on maximum effort to support the airborne landings at Arnhem and Nijmegen and given the task of bombing the military barracks at Ede, but bad weather hampered the operation until the 25th. When operations resumed aircraft of 98 Squadron attacked military targets but were met with fighter opposition; two Mitchells were shot down by Fw 190s, the first aircraft losses to fighters since the Wing was created. By the 26th the airborne forces were withdrawn. On 6th October another accident occurred when two Mitchells of 180 collided on take off, one crashing in Dunsfold village.

As the armies advanced fresh targets presented themselves. With the range becoming greater, No 139 Wing moved out to Belgium on 5th October, followed by the aircraft on the 17th. The airfield at Dunsfold was now on a care and maintenance basis and in the coming months the 28 armourers began to dispose of bombs left behind. During December 1944 British and American Transport Command used the base as an emergency landing ground, with as many as 20 Dakotas at a time arriving.

By the beginning of the New Year the German army's winter offensive had been halted in the Ardennes and the Allied forces were now poised to make the final decisive strike into Germany through France and the Low Countries. The squadrons in Europe would need all the support they could get from pilots and aircraft. On 7th January

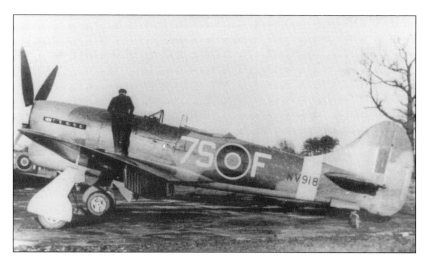

A Hawker Tempest of No 83 GSU, Dunsfold 1945. (Air Comm. J. W. Frost)

1945 No 83 Group (2nd Tactical Air Force) Flying Training Wing of No 83 Group Support Unit arrived at Dunsfold from Westhampnett with 100 officers and 160 men. Their function was to train and then ferry new pilots and repaired, modified or new aircraft to the Group's operational squadrons in Europe. Soon large stocks of aircraft built up, including Spitfires, Typhoons, Tempests and a few AOP Austers.

With all the activity, accidents happened. The first mishap occurred on 9th February when a Typhoon from the remainder of the 83 GSU at Westhampnett ran out of fuel and crashed on the outskirts of the airfield, killing the pilot. More followed. A Tempest's engine failed on take off and a Typhoon cartwheeled spectacularly down the runway when its brakes locked, but thankfully both pilots survived.

Dunsfold had now become a satellite of Odiham and in March No 83 GSU started its own communication flight using Ansons to ferry goods, equipment and new pilots to squadrons and bring back ferry pilots. Other aircraft, including Dakotas and Liberators, used the airfield for training, and as this continued more accidents occurred, though mainly with the high-powered Typhoon and Tempest aircraft. In March a detachment of No 60 MU returned to service aircraft on site.

With the end of the war in Europe now in sight, Dunsfold entered a new phase in its short history when it was designated an arrival centre for evacuated prisoners of war from north-west Europe. No 2 hangar was selected as the reception centre and was decked out with flowers

Dunsfold April to June 1945, taken from the control tower. Transport and ambulances parked outside one of the T2 type hangars when Short Stirlings were used to repatriate prisoners of war. (P. McCue)

and other decorations to welcome them home.

First it was a trickle, then on 21st April two aircraft arrived with 70 ex-POWs and the numbers began increasing daily. On the 22nd, 16 Stirlings brought back 346 repatriates, and on the 24th the largest number to have arrived so far, 38 Dakotas with 1,069 men. Throughout the coming weeks Stirlings, Dakotas, Lancasters and Halifaxes would fill the sky, circling about Dunsfold awaiting their turn to land. By the end of April over 3,000 repatriates had passed through. On 30th April a snowstorm reduced operations but two aircraft got through and the villagers of nearby Cranleigh sent fresh flowers to decorate the hangar. The rate increased and on 8th May, VE Day, 72 aircraft landed with 1,667 men. The end of the war in Europe was enthusiastically celebrated, several pilots spending the evening in the Crown at Chiddingfold while for those left on the camp a dance was organised in the cinema with free beer as the evening progressed. The next day a record 160 aircraft brought back 3,953 men. By the end of May a total of 44,474 men had been repatriated. The arrivals continued until 15th

June, when 1,500 Canadian soldiers arrived en route for home.

When the POW flights ended, No 83 GSU was still active training pilots for the continuing war in the Far East. Six Typhoons practising rocket attacks on a dispersal area near to the Compasses gate were diving when the engine note of one of them made people look up. One Typhoon was in a vertical dive, out of control, and though it turned slightly to miss some trees it hit the ground with a muffled explosion. The pilot had no chance of escape.

Dunsfold now had another change of role, losing its communications flight and receiving squadrons back from operational duties for disbandment. The first to arrive were the Canadian 401, 402 and 403 Squadrons, followed by Spitfires and Mosquitos. On 1st August 1945 Dunsfold became a satellite of Biggin Hill and No 83 GSU was renamed No 83 Group Disbandment Centre. Canadian squadrons, old friends, continued to return – 400, 414 and 430 with their Spitfires and Typhoons. The men were either sent home to Canada or went on to the Pacific theatre of war.

On 15th August the war in the Far East ended suddenly with the surrender of Japan and soon there was a noticeable lessening of activity at the airfield. By the end of September it had become busy once more, however, as squadrons of Typhoons arrived for disbandment – 121 Wing (175, 181 and 182 Squadrons) and No 122 Wing (486 RNZAF and 174 and 184 Squadrons). A sad sight, as over 100 Typhoons were parked in rows and, no longer required for service in the peacetime RAF, destined for scrap. In October No 83 GDC moved to Lasham for disbandment and to hand over to No 84 GDC who would look after any outstanding commitments. Further disbanding continued with No 88 Group returning from Norway where it had been employed reorganising the post-war Norwegian Air Force, and 667 Squadron was the last operational squadron to arrive for disbandment on 12th December 1945.

Dunsfold's future was now uncertain. In January 1946 it became part of Lasham and on 15th February it was transferred to Tangmere and should have ended its operational status. A variety of aircraft still used the station but on 2nd September it was transferred from 11 Group Fighter Command to 244 Group Technical Training Command.

There had been pressure from the local councils for the land to revert to agriculture but the RAF intended to retain the airfield. On 10th August 1946 it was made available for use by Skyways Ltd. Skyways soon became the biggest air charter company in Europe, operating a fleet of Dakotas, Skymasters, Yorks and Lancastrians, with the oil companies their biggest customers, and employing a workforce of 1,300 people and 350 aircrew. In August 1948 business increased further with the Yorks and Lancastrians employed on the Berlin Airlift.

Then in 1949 a series of crashes and the ending of the Berlin Airlift brought a change of fortune to the company and in 1950 Skyways Ltd went into voluntary liquidation and their aircraft were sold.

Dunsfold remained unoccupied until 1951 when Hawker were offered the use of the airfield on a long lease from the Ministry of Supply and took over the tenancy. Hawker wished to move from their grass airfield at Langley and Dunsfold was also convenient as the nearest airfield to their manufacturing site at Kingston. This began an association with a line of fine aircraft, including the Sea Hawk and the beautiful and successful Hunter.

In 1954, Rolls Royce at Hucknall had completed their trials of a revolutionary new engine, the Pegasus, which had vectored thrust. In 1957 Hawker conceived the idea of using this engine in a VSTOL aircraft. The aircraft, Project No. P1127, was constructed and successfully flown in the 'hover' position by Chief Test Pilot, Bill Bedford, in October 1960. It was to become the prototype for the outstanding Harrier line of aircraft. In 1963 the company became Hawker Siddely Aviation and, after many amalgamations and name changes, part of British Aerospace in 1974.

Today, Dunsfold also acts as an emergency diversion airfield for Gatwick Airport, as the main runway at over 2,000 metres is capable of accepting the largest aircraft in service, including a fully laden Boeing 747.

3
REDHILL

A delightful airfield set in beautiful Surrey countryside near to South Nutfield, Redhill was already extremely busy when war broke out in 1939. Since its inception in 1934 by British Air Transport as a landing area of 100 acres, the airfield had doubled in size through the purchase of adjoining land and the removal of the Nutfield sewage farm.

In March 1934 Redhill Flying Club was formed to train pupils to A and B licence standard and also in night flying. The fleet consisted of Gipsy Moths, two Puss Moths and a Leopard Moth. A year later BAT were awarded a contract to train Imperial Airways engineers for B licences and in basic flying skills. In addition, 3rd April 1935 saw Sir Alan Cobham open his National Aviation Day tour at Redhill in front of 3,000 people. Then, on 3rd July 1937, in accordance with a government proposal to open RAF reserve centres, No 15 Elementary & Reserve Flying Training School was formed at Redhill, to be controlled by BAT under Flying Officer A. G. Douglas RAFO as managing director. No 15 was a purely volunteer reserve unit as opposed to other schools which took short service commission entrants as well.

The first aircraft allocated were some weary DH 60 metal Gipsy Moths. Objections that they were unsuited to the small airfield were overruled by the Air Ministry and Reserve Command, and training commenced on schedule. The Gipsy Moths in fact gave sterling service and were only replaced by Miles Magisters some 15 months later after clocking up 3,997 hours. Two Hawker Harts were added in October 1937.

There was a great increase in flying in 1938 as the Reserve Flying

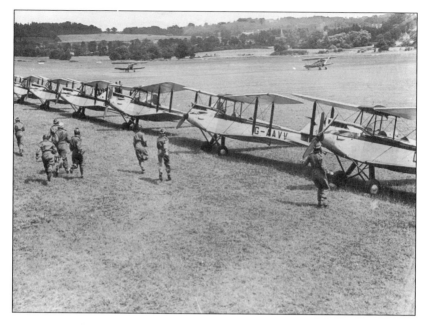

The ladies of the Civil Air Guard section of the Redhill Flying Club scramble to their waiting Gipsy Moths, 1939. Hawker Harts of the 15 ERFTS are in the background.

School expanded its activities and later in the year the Redhill Flying Club instituted pilot training under the new Civil Air Guard scheme. New buildings were needed, including a clubhouse for the 70 male and female CAG recruits, and a terrace of eight additional hangars had to be erected alongside King's Mill Lane to house all the additional aircraft. Alongside the old hangar a tall watch tower was built to oversee the airfield and control the increasing number of aircraft movements. By 1939 training commitments had increased still further – contracts were received to train 40 Short Service officers, the Voluntary Reserve pilots had increased to 200, and a fresh section to train 200 aircrew had been started. The school were eagerly awaiting delivery of their three Ansons.

Redhill also held a major air display on 29th July 1939, remarkable for the fact that large aircraft including an Imperial Airways Ensign and a Lufthansa Fw Condor landed and were displayed alongside RAF machines, including a Hurricane and a Wellington.

Then, on 3rd September 1939, war was declared and temporarily all flying at Redhill ceased. The training school had over the years collected 28 Magisters, 15 Hart variants, four Battles and three Ansons, plus another four Battles, six Tiger Moths and three Harts from 56 ERFTS which BAT had operated at Kenley for only ten days before war broke out; there were also 29 instructional staff and two Link trainers.

All serviceable aircraft were immediately ferried out as it was thought they were in danger, and the school was renamed No 15 Elementary Flying Training School. The Civil Air Guard ceased to exist and the flying club machines were overhauled and then impressed into service duties. Many of the CAG trained pilots went on for further training in the RAF and other men and women pilots saw distinguished service in the newly formed Air Transport Auxiliary ferrying aircraft from the manufacturers to service squadrons.

For the first few months of the war very little training was done but the Magisters soon returned and between 11th September and 6th November 1939, certain qualified pupils were given instructors courses. The following winter was gloomy and entirely inactive at Redhill except for the RAF guard of 15 men and a sergeant and a course of 34 volunteer recruits arriving on 20th November for an eight-week refresher course.

1940 began with the mobilisation of all flying personnel into the RAF. Flying Officer Douglas was promoted to Squadron Leader and became the commanding officer and chief flying instructor but the maintenance, ground school and accounts at Redhill retained their civilian status.

On 1st March 1940 a course was started for 'testing and grading' the Polish pilot officers who had found their way to Britain after the fall of Poland. The idea was to judge their capabilities before sending them to an Operational Training Unit, as their experience varied and many had not flown a more sophisticated aircraft than the Battle trainers they were using. The airmen were stationed at Eastchurch and the first course commenced under their commanding officer, Group Captain Davidson.

The Polish Grading School was independent of the Flying Training School and had its own small fleet of Magisters and three Fairey Battle trainers. With this further increase in flying, the aerodrome at Penshurst, also on the main railway line, was used as a relief landing ground on a detachment basis, and at Newchapel an emergency landing ground was sited. Nevertheless, one pupil landed at the decoy airfield at Lullingstone and the instructor had the job of extricating the Magister from between the obstacles and barbed wire!

The first three courses, each of 15 Polish airmen, were soon well

53

Miles Magisters and a Fairey Battle of 15 EFTS and the Polish Grading School prepare for another day's flying training, 1940. Taken from the control tower. (C. Nepean Bishop)

under way under the direction of Squadron Leader Wallace, who came from Eastchurch and was responsible for laying down the training schedules before he moved on to Hucknall as chief flying instructor of the first Polish Operational Training Unit. The pupils were extremely hard-working, with a burning desire to take the war back to the enemy, but the language barrier was to prove extremely difficult during the training. Their flying was a little rusty, but this was only to be expected from men who had not flown for some time.

Each pilot flew ten hours on Magisters and 15 hours on Battles. As the war developed the shortage of CFS instructors became acute and the more experienced pupils who spoke English stayed behind to train as instructors for further courses.

In May the situation in Europe worsened when Denmark and the Low Countries were invaded. The airfield defences were strengthened and a platoon of the South Staffordshire Regiment arrived to add to the force. The flying school was split up into flights as staff and pupils

54

Pilots of the Polish Grading School relax in front of the old 15 ERFTS wooden building, 1940. (C. Nepean Bishop)

began to dig trenches and train in the use of machine guns and small arms.

Two months earlier, C. Nepean Bishop ('Bish'), the well known pre-war Brooklands pilot and keen photographer, had been posted to 15 EFTS as an instructor with B flight. Towards the end of May he recorded that the hitherto relatively peaceful skies over Surrey were now full of aircraft passing to and from France, including the many transport aircraft such as Ensigns and Harrows, escorted by fighters, bringing squadron personnel back across the Channel. The sound of distant gunfire could be heard and by the end of the month, when flying over the main railway from the coast nearby, the line was seen to be full of trains packed with troops of the British Expeditionary Force returning from France through the Dunkirk evacuation.

Times were bad and on 1st June the Commanding Officer was summoned to Flying Training Command and told to evacuate 15 EFTS and the Polish Grading School immediately to Carlisle. On 3rd June the schools left Redhill and 16 Squadron arrived with their Westland Lysanders. Formation flying had been forbidden at Redhill but when all the school's fleet of aircraft moved out, they flew line astern, an instructor leading each flight.

The Lysanders of 16 Squadron did not stay long. They had flown in from Lympne where they had been employed dropping vital supplies for the beleaguered garrison at Calais. The men pitched their tents alongside their aircraft and left after two weeks, the airfield now becoming the base for No 50 Army Co-operation Wing.

The general situation was grim. The civilian population had been warned to prepare for invasion and on 18th June the Prime Minister, Mr Winston Churchill, warned the nation: '... the battle of France is over. I expect that the Battle of Britain is about to begin.'

It was on 10th July 1940 that the air battles began in earnest and that is accepted as the first official day of the Battle of Britain. A Dornier 17 reconnaissance aircraft, escorted by Me 109s, spotted a British convoy in the Channel heading for the South Coast ports and immediately radioed its position to base. Picked up on radar, the Dornier and Me 109s were soon intercepted and a fierce air battle ensued. The Germans, now aware of the presence of the convoy, also sent massed fighter and bomber formations to attack and the battle raged throughout the day.

Hitler's invasion plan demanded air superiority and with it the complete destruction of Fighter Command. These attacks on Channel shipping and ports were intended to draw the RAF into the air for this purpose and when it failed the attacks switched inland.

On 12th August 1940, the eve of 'Adler Tag' or Eagle Day, the date set for the invasion of England, mammoth fleets of German aircraft attacked the radar stations and airfields along the South Coast, and on 15th August turned inland, when it was the turn of Croydon. Yet with air battles raging overhead, Redhill remained inactive and almost untouched. No 50 Army Co-operation Wing had moved out and Redhill became a satellite of Kenley, providing an alternative landing ground for use by aircraft whose own airfield was temporarily unserviceable due to enemy attack. After the Croydon raid the comparative quiet of the airfield was momentarily shattered when an Me 110 of Erpro 210 was shot down by Sergeant Dymond of 111 Squadron and Sergeant Pearce of 32 Squadron crash landed, his plane disintegrating on the airfield.

When the Luftwaffe realised the RAF could not be beaten into submission, daylight raids diminished and the night bombing raids began on London and other cities. Night fighter operations began as part of the counter measures and Redhill was chosen as a forward base for a detachment of No 600 Squadron with their Blenheim IVfs and a new Beaufighter If equipped with Airborne Interception Radar. As

A Gladiator of 615 Squadron returning from France calls at Redhill en route for Kenley or Croydon, 1940. (C. Nepean Bishop)

more Beaufighter replacements arrived, conversion to the new aircraft was carried out by day whilst operations continued at night. Difficulties were soon found in operating the new, more powerful Beaufighter from a small slippery grass airfield, and at night Redhill had no navigational aids – the runway lighting was only glim lamps and gooseneck paraffin flares and a mobile Chance light. Accommodation for personnel had improved from under canvas to billeting out but the mess hall was still a marquee on the airfield.

In early October, 600 Squadron left to be replaced by 219 Squadron with their Blenheim IVfs, who also took over the 600 Squadron Beaufighters. Once again the training consisted of conversion by day and flying operational patrols at night, which was proving hazardous. In early October 600 Squadron had lost a Blenheim with engine failure in heavy rain, crashing at Forest Row and killing all the crew. October was also a tragic month for 219 Squadron, losing a Blenheim with engine failure which crashed at Ewhurst, although one crew member baled out successfully. Two Beaufighters were lost – one crashed near

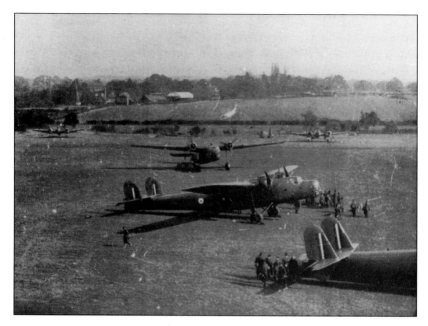

Handley Page Harrows and Bristol Bombays disembark men and equipment of 219 Squadron in front of the control tower, October 1940. Note the Beaufighters in the background. (Imperial War Museum)

Woking but the crew parachuted to safety, while the other went down near Balcombe Place in bad visibility, hitting a tree; the crew were tragically all killed.

The early Airborne Interception Radar sets left a lot to be desired and no successes were claimed. As autumn wore on the wet grass and mists made Redhill inoperable on some nights and so Kenley made arrangements for a flight to stand by in case it was required. 219 Squadron also found Tangmere more suited to Beaufighter operation and by the end of December had moved south, leaving Redhill empty.

Redhill now fell quiet in the winter but the carefree life enjoyed by the men was shattered by the appearance of a Station Warrant Officer who soon had the 'spit and polish' back again! In January work began on a north/south runway and the laying of Sommerfeld steel mesh tracking on both runways, along with a perimeter track. With these improvements, and more envisaged, in February the airfield was upgraded in status to RAF Redhill, whose fortunes now were very much allied to the parent airfield at RAF Kenley.

On 1st May 1941, with the airfield conditions much improved, No 1 Squadron under the command of Squadron Leader Brooker, and part of the Kenley Wing, moved in from Croydon with their Hurricane IIas where they had been employed as a specialist night fighter unit. On the night of 10th May came one of the last major raids of the Blitz on London. A force of 550 German bombers raided the capital in perfect weather conditions and 1 Squadron were soon in action with 13 Hurricanes. Without the advantage of AI Radar they had to rely on visual interception, guided only by approximate GCI Radar plots and by observing AA activity and searchlights. In the brilliant moonlight they shot down six enemy aircraft, one probable and two damaged. Three fell to the guns of Czech Sergeant Josef Dygryn (two He 111s and a Ju 88), while Frenchman J. Demozay, Squadron Leader Brooker and Flying Officer Jackman each claimed a Heinkel and Czech Sergeant Kratkoruky damaged another. The night's work was marred by the loss of Czech Pilot Officer Behal whose Hurricane was shot down and crashed in Selsdon Park. Overall, Fighter Command destroyed 30 enemy aircraft.

No 1 Squadron stayed at Redhill until 1st June when they changed places with another Hurricane squadron from Kenley, 258, and then returned on 14th June. This corresponded with a visit from the Air Officer Commanding in Chief, Fighter Command, Air Marshal Sir W. Sholto Douglas KCB, MC, DFC, whose policy of 'leaning forward into France' and taking the fight to the enemy, was soon to be practised by the Redhill squadrons as part of the Kenley Wing.

No 1 Squadron commenced the Circus operations that were to be a major part of the Kenley Wing's forays into France in the coming months by acting as escort to six Blenheims, sent to attack Desvres aerodrome. 'Circus' operations provided the many types of fighter cover to small formations of bombers attacking short-range targets in north-west France, the prime object being to draw enemy fighters up to the attack. On the return a furious scrap ensued and four Me 109s were destroyed. Offensive sweeps over the Channel and northern France continued until the end of the month when 1 Squadron left Redhill.

The Kenley Wing now exchanged their Hurricanes for Spitfires for all coming offensive operations. The three squadrons forming the Kenley Wing were 452 (RAAF), 485 (RNZAF), and 602 (City of Glasgow). In the next eight months the squadrons would be rotated, each one carrying out a spell of duty at Redhill, the other two at Kenley.

485 Squadron's publicly funded Spitfire Vbs, July-October 1941. (Imperial War Museum)

The first Spitfire squadron to be posted to Redhill was 485 of the Royal New Zealand Air Force under the command of Squadron Leader M. W. B. Knight. Conditions at the airfield had improved considerably with the pilots now billeted in a large country mansion when off duty. There were also plenty of local recreational facilities to occupy the pilots when not flying.

Straight away, 485 was heavily engaged, sometimes flying two operations a day. The small formations of Blenheims and Stirlings they accompanied attacked targets in the Bethune, Albert, Cherbourg, Le Touquet and Hazebrouck areas and industrial targets in the mouth of the Seine, prompting heavy response by the Me 109s.

In July, 485 flew 22 of the 33 Circus operations mounted by the Kenley Wing as well as other escort duties. By the end of the month they had destroyed four Me 109s, three by Flight Lieutenant Wells and one by Pilot Officer Stewart, but sadly three pilots were missing.

On the ground the threat of invasion was still being taken seriously and on the night of 7th July, two Whitleys brought paratroops to take up position outside the airfield. A full-scale exercise was undertaken to test the airfield's defences against such an attack. The airfield guard at this time was the Princess Patricia's Canadian Light Infantry.

August 1941 began with escort duties and on the 12th, 485 was ordered as target cover for six Hampdens on a Circus to Gosnay. The Hampdens were joined at a rendezvous above Manston, then the group crossed the French coast at 25,000 feet. The Hampdens completed their bombing operation and on the way back twelve Me 109s were spotted and a large-scale scrap ensued. Five pilots fired short bursts but were unable to see with what results. One Me 109 was damaged but two 485 Spitfires were also damaged and one pilot was reported missing. The pilots were now at a disadvantage when engaged over enemy territory. Baling-out or forced landing meant capture or at best landing in the Channel. Also, the enemy fighters could choose their moments to attack, often with the advantage of height and their backs to the sun.

August also saw 485's first encounters with the new Fw 190s but to help counter this, replacements arrived for the ageing Spitfire Mk IIs. They came in the form of the improved Mk V with cannon, each aircraft publicly funded by subscriptions from different New Zealand provinces and bearing their names. A high level visit to Redhill on 13th August included the 11 Group Commander, Air Marshal Sir Trafford L. Leigh-Mallory, and the Prime Minister of New Zealand, the Rt Hon Peter Fraser. There was a shortage of pilots from New Zealand and the Prime Minister asked several of the more experienced men if they would consider returning home to train new pilots. However, all those approached said they wished to remain here.

The Circus operations continued through September. On the 18th the Kenley Wing formed up with another wing over Beachy Head and escorted Blenheims to attack a power station at Rouen. There was heavy bombing on the target and moderate flak but on the return journey they came under continuous attack by 50 Me 109s. Leaving the attack until the fighters turned for home was quite common. The fighting was fierce and eight enemy fighters were claimed by Fighter Command, three by 485, but six Spitfires were lost, one from 485.

The operations scaled down slightly in October and on the 21st, 485 flew its final fighter sweep to St Omer and in the afternoon moved to Kenley. During their stay at Redhill they had destroyed 14 enemy aircraft, plus eight probables and nine damaged, but lost ten pilots.

On 24th October, 452 flew in from Kenley for their spell of duty at Redhill under the command of Squadron Leader R. W. Bungay, the first Australian squadron to be based at the airfield. Different in temperament to the more reserved New Zealanders, they enjoyed in their off duty hours travelling up to London to their favourite haunts.

On one occasion they recruited a couple of buskers on the way, taking them to a London hotel and passing them off as the squadron band! Operations continued for the rest of October, mainly Rodeo fighter sweeps over St Omer, Mardyke, Calais and Cap Gris Nez. In November and December operations continued as weather permitted and in this period twelve enemy aircraft were destroyed.

This year Christmas was a festive affair at Redhill, made possible by the completion of the communal complex and the new NAAFI. The weather experienced at this time restricted operations but on 9th January 1942, two aircraft led by Flight Lieutenant Smith led a successful small-scale fighter attack (known as a Rhubarb) on an alcohol distillery at Colville, the last operation before the squadron moved out, returning to Kenley on the 14th. They were replaced by 602 (City of Glasgow) Squadron from Kenley led by Squadron Leader A. C. Deere DFC. The weather deteriorated, heavy snow falling and curtailing operations further, and on the 27th came a change of command when Squadron Leader B. E. Finucane DSO, DFC and Bar took over from Deere.

The weather and airfield conditions improved sufficiently so that on 12th February, twelve Spitfires of 602 were able to join an operation with 452 and 485 mounted by the Kenley Wing. However, the Beauforts they were meant to escort could not be seen and so the Wing proceeded alone over the Channel and found destroyers and E-boats on the move, which they attacked. What they had come across was the vanguard of the German fleet, the battleships *Scharnhorst*, *Gneisenau* and *Prinz Eugen* making their break from Brest (see Kenley).

On the 14th, 602 left for Kenley, temporarily, and on the 20th two aircraft were led by Finucane on a Jim Crow operation – a patrol of the home coastline to intercept any hostile aircraft crossing the coast. Finucane was flying down the French coast when he spotted two Fw 190s taking off from Mardyke. They immediately made a head-on attack. Finucane's plane was hit by the first bursts and he ordered Pilot Officer Lewis home. However, the Fw 190s followed and he turned to protect his leader. One Fw 190 crashed into the sea and the other broke off. Finucane and Lewis returned to Kenley and the Squadron Leader made a perfect landing despite his wounds.

On 25th February, 602 returned from Kenley. In March they carried out one further operation with 485, a patrol over Le Touquet. A number of enemy aircraft were seen and heavy flak was encountered off Calais. Sergeant Strudwick's aircraft was hit by cannon shell, damaging the starboard aileron and flap. He crash-landed on the aerodrome and although his aircraft was destroyed, he escaped unhurt.

On 5th March 1942, 602 went back to Kenley and 452 returned to Redhill. On the ground there was a large-scale gas practice. There was always a great fear of gas attacks and frequent exercises were mounted whereby personnel would carry out their duties wearing respirators for considerable periods of time.

Three Circus operations were flown in the next week. On the 9th, six Bostons were escorted in an attack on a power station at Mazingarbe; 452 flew at 11,000 feet and two Me 109s were destroyed, with one damaged.

On the 13th, twelve Bostons attacked the marshalling yards at Hazebrouck, with Kenley Wing as high cover. Then on the 14th, twelve Spitfires of the Kenley Wing were leaving the target after escorting twelve Bostons, when they were attacked by enemy aircraft. Two Fw 190s were destroyed.

The 20th March saw the departure of 452 Squadron from Redhill and the Kenley Wing, to be replaced by another Australian squadron, 457. They were led by their British commanding officer, Squadron Leader P. M. Brothers, DFC, who later recalled those first days at Redhill:

'After a weather-induced chaotic move from the Isle of Man, 457 Squadron arrived at Redhill on 23rd March 1942, eager for action. It was not long coming. On 26th, with 602 and 485 Squadrons from Kenley, the Wing took part in Ramrod 17 escorting bombers attacking Le Havre. Engaged by Me 109s, appropriately as CO, I was fortunate enough to score the squadron's first kill but saddened by our first loss, P/O Jerry Halse.

'So we settled into our new routine; sweeps over France on the 27th and two on the 28th, the second bringing disaster during a large dogfight with the loss of our Sector Commander and CO Kenley, Group Captain Victor Beamish, DSO & Bar, DFC, AFC. Having latched on to a Me 109 he was warned of another on his tail and replied, typically, "I will fix this one first". The loss of such a successful and distinguished leader was a great blow. His replacement, and I believe the only man with the qualities necessary to succeed him, Group Captain R. L. R. (Batchy) Atcherley, CB, AFC & Bar, visited us on the 5th April, landing in his inimitable way on the perimeter track and rolling to a stop outside my office door.'

Sometimes his Australian airmen were a little boisterous:

'Whilst daily operations continued, so did nightly social visits to Redhill and Reigate. To ensure that my airmen had a good but not too good a time, I had formed a volunteer Town Picket of six men and a

A Spitfire of 457 Squadron landing while another stands at readiness with 'Trolley-Acc' plugged in, March 1942. (Imperial War Museum)

Corporal, armed with axe-helves and a truck. Came the night when two Army 'Redcaps' (Royal Corps of Military Police) made the mistake of arresting two of my airmen for being "improperly dressed" – having their jackets undone and caps off, only to find themselves picked up by the Town Picket, knocked on the head, thrown in the truck, brought back and locked in our Guardroom, bootlaces and braces removed for their own protection in accordance with regulations. I was visited next day by an irate Redcap colonel demanding their release. He was not amused to be told that any Brit who laid a hand on my Aussies would get the same treatment.'

602 Squadron, led by Squadron Leader B. E. Finucane, moved into Redhill on 13th May to form, with 457, the Redhill Wing. Later that month the Australians returned home to fight the Japanese. They were relieved by 402, the first Canadian squadron to be based at Redhill. Alongside 602, the two squadrons flew many mixed operations. In mid June Finucane was promoted to Wing Commander and moved to take over the Hornchurch Wing, while Brothers returned to Redhill to

64

Squadron Leader P. M. Brothers, DFC, who commanded 457 Squadron at Redhill and Kenley, and later 602 Squadron at Redhill. (Air Commodore P. M. Brothers CBE, DSO, DFC)

A line-up of Focke-Wulf FW 190s. (MAP)

command 602 Squadron.

On 1st July it was felt that something big was afoot when several Harrows of Transport Command arrived and offloaded the servicing echelon of 308 (Polish), 310 and 312 (Czech) Squadrons of 10 Group, to be followed by the squadrons' aircraft. The airfield was now bulging at the seams.

The aircraft had arrived painted with black and white recognition stripes ready to take part in some secret offensive exercise, but on the 6th the exercise was cancelled and the three squadrons moved back to the Exeter area.

Redhill had now become an important forward staging post for visiting squadrons to stay for a while when carrying out special missions. This made for greater awareness of the danger from enemy attack and defence exercises were regularly mounted. The parachute and cable AA system was still in readiness (both Kenley and Biggin Hill systems were fired during the earlier raids) and a practice launch was mounted. Disconcertingly, one rocket failed to ignite and several of the other seven did not reach the required height.

In mid July came another change. 602 moved to Peterhead and 611 replaced them, commanded by Squadron Leader D. H. Watkins, DFC and in the process of re-equipping with Spitfire Mk IXs.

66

Sergeant/Pilot M. A. Liskutin inspects his damaged Spitfire Vb, 19th August 1942.
(Sqn Ldr M. A. Liskutin DFC, AFC)

Until the end of the month there were many Rhubarb operations flown against railways and other communication systems in north-west France and at the end of July 402 took part in an Army Co-operation exercise. Code-named Operation Harold, it consisted of 'attacking' armoured columns at Lamberhurst, Rolvenden and Cranbrook.

The Belgian squadron No 350 arrived, led by Squadron Leader D. A.

Guillaume, DFC and the following month saw convoy patrols and escort duties for Flying Fortresses attacking targets in Germany. 402 began receiving their own Spitfire IXs the counter to the Fw 190s. On 13th and 14th August, 402 and 611 left for Kenley to take part in an exercise and on the 15th, 303 (Polish), 310 and 312 (Czech) Squadrons returned to Redhill to join 350. With the number of aircraft and tents dispersed, the airfield was once again bulging at the seams.

On 17th August 1942, 350, 310 and 312 Squadrons, flying Circus No 202, escorted Fortress bombers to Rouen, Dunquerque and Cherbourg and on the 18th, the same squadrons left Redhill on a feint Rodeo to Berck-sur-Mer and down the coast to Le Treport. No enemy aircraft were seen and all returned safely. On return the squadrons were given a preliminary briefing for the following day's operations and restricted to camp for the night.

Next morning at dawn pilots from 303, 310, 312 and 350 Squadrons were in the dispersal tent at 5 am for briefing. They were to fly as escort to 'Hurribombers' attacking shipping in Boulogne harbour and the Channel up to Dieppe. All aircraft had black and white recognition stripes painted on wings and fuselage. The flak was worse than ever but the attack was successful with no losses and on the way home several E-boats were attacked. After debriefing at Redhill it was a quick cup of tea whilst the aircraft were refuelled and rearmed ready for the next sortie.

Sergeant M. A. Liskutin (later Squadron Leader Liskutin DFC, AFC) flew with 310 (Czech) Squadron in support of Operation Jubilee, the Dieppe raid. He records that the next sortie was to fly at sea level cross-Channel, then climb to 8,000 feet and patrol a line to the south and east of Dieppe, intercepting any enemy aircraft before they reached the bridgehead or Allied ships.

It was mid-morning and already troops were seen to be pulling out of the burning town of Dieppe. The patrol line was established flying line abreast and after the first about turn the sector controller warned of the presence of enemy aircraft in the vicinity. Soon after, Liskutin spotted Fw 190s and reported, 'Tally-ho, bandits at two o'clock high' as he climbed to attack. Two Fw 190s came in for a head-on attack, swerved, and Liskutin closed in on the second. Checking behind, he spotted another on his tail and with a quick evasive zig-zag had the aircraft in his sights. His guns hit the target on his right wing. Almost immediately, his own aircraft was hit.

A quick flick roll was followed by a spin down to 4,000 feet. The aircraft was controllable but there was a gaping hole in the right wing and the left aileron was badly damaged. Liskutin turned the aircraft towards the smoke over Dieppe and realised that he could fly straight, but only by exerting great pressure on the control column to give maximum aileron deflection. After a short while the physical strain of holding the aircraft in level flight became unbearable, but the day was saved by jamming his refuelling crowbar in the fuselage and against the control column. He then gave a thought to how and where he could land the aircraft. At 2,000 feet and at about 200 mph the aircraft appeared to fly straight but now stalled at about 160 mph. This meant an approach and landing above this speed and without the damaged flaps!

Liskutin decided to press on to Redhill where an accurate approach and landing was made, the aircraft touching down at nearly 165 mph and zig-zagging before being pulled up safely without any further damage. After debriefing he was offered a rest but declined as a spare Spitfire, DU-O, was available. It was fortunate that Vickers had a Spitfire repair shop for his own aircraft, DU-V, in No 1 hangar.

The final sortie for 312 that day was to patrol over Dieppe and a convoy of Allied ships. It was not long after taking up the patrol at 2,000 feet that Dornier 217s came out of lowering cloud. Liskutin gave the customary 'Tally-ho' giving their position, and aimed at full power for the nearest bomber. His first burst of cannon fire knocked off the astro-dome and the second set the starboard engine on fire. A final long burst sent the Dornier into the waves. Climbing away to rejoin the rest of the squadron, another Do 217 was spotted but Liskutin had run out of ammunition. A fresh squadron of Spitfires had arrived and following his call, sent the Dornier into the sea.

Next day 312 returned to Harrowbeer, and the other squadrons to their own airfields whilst 611 Squadron returned from Kenley to Redhill. During Operation Jubilee, Fighter Command had flown 2,339 sorties. The squadrons operating from Redhill destroyed 24 enemy aircraft with seven probables for the loss of two Spitfires and two pilots.

On 23rd September, 350 Squadron left for Southend and 611 Squadron with its servicing echelon moved to Biggin Hill, to be replaced by two Canadian squadrons. In flew 412 from Tangmere and 416 from Martlesham and once again Redhill was host to a lively bunch of Canadians.

As autumn and winter approached operations continued, mainly escorting Fortresses and Bostons on bombing missions and attacking railway systems in northern France. Walrus amphibians were also protected on air-sea rescue work.

The winter was wet and windy and the station log reports that parts of the aerodrome were flooded. The Canadian airmen were billeted a few miles away and they were introduced to the joys of cycling. They soon adapted to this form of transport but the dark and slippery lanes of winter resulted in more than a few cuts and bruises. The winter had its compensations though, with parties and dances held in the NAAFI and WAAFs billeted in Nutfield Priory.

Early in the new year of 1943, the airfield, with 412 and 416 Squadrons took part in Exercise Spartan, a 15-day army close support exercise involving hurried moves of bases and low strafing attacks on army units. Redhill became the headquarters of Z Group (representing a Tactical Air Force) in one of the biggest exercises mounted so far in preparation for the coming invasion. No 62 LAA battery, 11 Regiment RCA, arrived with six Bofors guns, all the additional personnel creating an accommodation problem.

In February, 416 moved to Kenley, and 421 replaced them in March, while in April 412 arrived from Kenley as an additional squadron.

By 1943 it was expected by everyone that the Allies would return in force to Europe – but where and precisely when? A combined service operation of such magnitude by land, sea and air would demand the ultimate in planning. In the air the support would be required from a specialist air force both for the invading forces and to follow the advancing armies, similar to the 1st Tactical Air Force so successfully employed in the North African landings and up into Sicily and Italy. It was at this time that the 2nd Tactical Air Force was envisaged. This special force would be drawn from Fighter, Bomber and Transport Commands, essentially mobile and able to operate from makeshift airfields as the armies advanced. Initially it would operate from temporary advanced airfields close to the south coast. To cope with this various operating procedures and training exercises were carried out at Redhill.

In May 1943, 421 was replaced by 401, another Canadian squadron, which soon converted to the clipped wing Spitfire V, designed for low level operation. The squadron then realised their role was to be in close support. A programme of low flying was started in a special area to the south-west of the aerodrome. After each low level pass the aircraft would climb, but some of the more high-spirited pilots pressed on at low level to surprise the assembled troops at a large Canadian Army Training Camp nearby, scattering all and sundry and much to the consternation of men and officers! Another scheme investigated, for use in the invasion, was to have aircraft carriers stationed near to the beachheads to allow aircraft to take off and land before airfields had been established. Two squadrons were selected for simulated deck landing training on a marked-out strip on the runway under the direction of a naval officer acting as batman. It was unpopular and not very successful but some pilots of 411 who became adept went on to Macrihanish in Scotland for further practice.

By this time there were about 800 personnel at Redhill and the number of bicycles had increased accordingly. Huge piles could be seen parked outside the mess halls and if lucky a better bicycle might be had when collecting!

During the summer of 1943 the 2nd Tactical Air Force began assembling, drawing on the squadrons from the various commands. It was comprised of four groups – 83 and 84 as the strike squadrons, 85 for the defence of the armies and 2 for the light/medium day bombers. Fighter Command by November 1943 had lost two thirds of its squadrons to the 2nd TAF and reverted to its old name of the Air Defence of Great Britain.

In July the three Canadian squadrons in residence at Redhill – 401, 411 and 412 – were formed into No 126 Airfield (Biggin Hill), 83 Group, 2nd TAF, retaining their old servicing echelons plus additional personnel from No 3207 Servicing Commando. In preparation for the rigours ahead, servicing was carried out in the open and everyone was in tented accommodation. The Airfield stayed at Redhill until 5th August when it moved out to one of the new Advanced Landing Grounds at Staplehurst in Kent, taking one flight of RAF Regiment No 2828 Squadron, with one flight of Bofors guns and one flight of Browning machine guns, for airfield defence.

In September, 131 and 504 Squadrons ADGB moved in and briefly formed a Redhill wing under Wing Commander Malfroy, joining with the USAF fighters in escorting American bombers on raids over France. They also took part in Operation Starkey, a feint attack on the Pas de Calais area to bring up the Luftwaffe fighters and destroy as many as possible, though the ploy did not work this time. They left Redhill on 17th and 18th September for Church Fenton and Castletown.

The airfield now became an unofficial landing ground for aircraft in distress, although efforts were made where possible to divert them as the runways had taken a pounding in the heavy flying and wet weather. On 15th September, two Fortresses and a Liberator landed, short of fuel. On the 23rd, Redhill was reduced to care and maintenance status.

In October several squadrons flew in to spend the winter, including No 128 Airfield (231, 400 and 414 Squadrons) with their Mustang Is, part of No 39 Reconnaissance Wing together with No 1 Casualty Evacuation Unit, 2nd TAF. The following month, 83 Group, 2nd TAF Communication Flight was formed to ferry officers around the country using a variety of aircraft including Lockheed Hudsons, Airspeed Oxfords, Percival Proctors and a Piper Cub.

414 Squadron returned to No 129 Airfield, Gatwick, which was now part of No 39 Reconnaissance Wing. In December, Mustangs of No 128 Airfield (231 and 400 Squadrons) carried out photo-reconnaissance over north-west France, and 400 was forced to spend some time at Kenley whilst essential repairs were carried out on the main runways.

At the end of the year work commenced on the only Advanced Landing Ground in Surrey, at Horne about four miles to the south-east of the airfield. Redhill was to be the parent airfield and all the meetings associated with Horne were dealt with there. On 30th December 1943, No 4749 Flight of 5004 Works Squadron arrived at Redhill, comprising one warrant officer and 52 airmen, to begin work on the new airfield. They were billeted along the ridge at Nutfield and taken to Redhill for breakfast before travelling by coach to Horne.

The end of the year saw the resumption for a time of night air attacks on London and other cities by the Luftwaffe. The new year of 1944 began very cold, but as the weather improved the squadrons of 39 Reconnaissance Wing were busy with their Mustangs photographing areas in north-west Europe for use in the coming invasion, and the secret-weapon launching sites.

By the end of February most overwintering squadrons had departed. The airfield was still concerned about the likelihood of airborne attacks and on 13th February, Operation Rebound was mounted when No 2741 AA Squadron, RAF Regiment 'defended' the airfield against paratroops, assumed to have landed a mile away, and attacks by low flying aircraft. On 20th February, a Flying Fortress force-landed with two engines on fire and the co-pilot was killed, and on the 23rd, in one of the renewed air raids, hundreds of incendiary bombs fell on three sides of the airfield, but none on the airfield itself.

In line with the policy of the 2nd TAF, No 83 Support Group was formed at the airfield from 1st to 7th March, Nos 405 and 410 Aircraft Repair Flights arriving from Detling to join with Nos 403 and 409 already at the airfield. They were soon busy servicing and repairing aircraft and were later joined by No 3207 Servicing Commando preparing new aircraft, mainly Typhoons, for squadron service. On 1st

April No 84 Group Communications Squadron replaced No 83.

During the war Redhill was the designated airfield for the local Air Training Corps Squadrons and Brian Buss, a cadet with 1408 Squadron, Dorking was a regular visitor to train and gain flight experience. On 30th April 1944, he was flying with other cadets in a DH Dominie and on take-off flew in a southerly direction. After a few minutes at about a thousand feet he looked down to see a grass field with two intersecting runways with a stream of clipped-wing Spitfires landing. Following them was another squadron. What he witnessed was the arrival of two of the three squadrons that would be operating from Horne in the next couple of days. He also recalls Redhill stacked with all types of aircraft. Spitfires, Typhoons and Hudsons were packed into every part of the airfield with only the runways left clear.

Stores and equipment were being built up at the airfield and in units in the surrounding countryside ready for the invasion of Europe. On 6th June 1944 the Allies invaded France in the biggest combined service operation ever mounted and Horne's aircraft were kept busy until they moved out on the 19th.

On 13th June, the first pilotless aircraft, Hitler's Vergeltungswaffen ('weapon of reprisal'), codenamed 'Diver', landed in Kent. First a few, then they came by the hundred. Fighter Command (ADGB) was sorely tested as it had been engaged in the Normandy landings since 6th June. However, a contingency plan had been formulated to deal with the V1s – first a belt of fighters, then AA guns, and finally a belt of barrage balloons across the North Downs from Cobham in Kent to Limpsfield in Surrey. Later the AA guns moved to the coast and the fighters operated to seaward of the guns and also behind. The balloon curtain was then increased by a further 750 balloons and now encompassed Redhill and Horne. On 30th June, Redhill became No 24 Balloon Centre and all landings were forbidden at both airfields. Several V1s flew over the airfield daily and on 10th July one exploded nearby.

The balloon barrage was essential to defence against the V1 but it was also a hazard to aircraft which had to navigate between them in set access lanes. On 6th August, a Dakota hit a balloon cable and lost six feet of its wing, which landed on nearby houses. The Dakota landed safely at RAF Gatwick.

The V1 attacks continued until the launching sites had been overrun. The airfield remained busy servicing and repairing aircraft and in September, No 16 Calibration Flight moved in, their task to assist in the calibration of AA guns and radar. In December the airfield became the base for the Canadian Casualty Evacuation Unit whose Dakotas flew in day and night, the wounded being transported to Smallfields Hospital, until they moved out in the New Year.

On 15th January 1945 Redhill became a satellite of Biggin Hill and in February the last squadrons to occupy the airfield were Nos 166 and 287 (AC). Soon they moved out and the airfield was quiet except for No 36 Maintenance Unit who had the task of moving the vast quantities of bombs which had been stored there.

British Air Transport returned in January 1947 and the airfield soon began to buzz with activity once again. Tiltman Langley Laboratories moved into the original hangar and later took over the squash court building and old clubhouse for their premises as consulting engineers in the aircraft and engineering industries. They carried out design and research work for most of the major aircraft companies, including Vickers Supermarine on the Swift and A. V. Roe on the Vulcan. The next hangar was occupied by Miles Aircraft and another housed the Chelsea College of Aeronautics.

The Redhill Flying Club also reopened, along with other clubs, and private owners returned. Many private aircraft had been impressed into service during the war and there was now a shortage of suitable types. Several ex-RAF and army planes were purchased including Tiger Moths, Moth Minors, Magisters and Austers. Amongst the interesting planes to be seen at Redhill were the Planet Satellite, an all-magnesium alloy pusher aircraft built at the Redwing factory in Croydon and erected at Redhill in 1948, and the Zaunköenig V2 G-ALUA, an 'unstallable' parasol-wing aircraft. Captured from the Germans, it was purchased by the Ultra-Light Aircraft Association and flown at Redhill by the Experimental Flying Group.

On 1st April 1948, No 15 Reserve Flying School reopened with six Tiger Moths and three instructors. The aircraft were maintained by British Air Transport and by 1949 the number had increased to 24, followed by six Anson XXIs and two Oxfords. In 1951 the Tiger Moths were replaced by Chipmunks, but on 30th April 1954 the school, and all others, closed. Gliding also took place at Redhill and the North Downs Gliding Trust (formerly Surrey Gliding Club) flew for a time at the airfield.

The end of an era came on 30th April 1954 when Redhill airfield closed, only Tiltman Langley Laboratories remaining until 1957. Redhill Flying Club moved to Croydon and became Surrey Flying Club, and when Croydon closed in 1959 they moved to Biggin Hill and became the Surrey and Kent Flying Club.

The airfield remained closed, although some flying took place, until

1959 when the Tiger Club arrived, followed by Bristow Helicopters in 1960 who set up their headquarters on the site. Bristows are now the biggest UK operators of helicopters and have pilot training and engineering schools on the site. The present Redhill Flying Club, now called Redhill Aviation, started in 1984 and there are other clubs on the airfield. Today, Redhill is a busy light aircraft centre and heliport.

4
CROYDON

In 1938, at the time of the Munich crisis, Croydon was the official 'Air Terminus of London', at the height of its fame. Since its modernisation in 1928, it had become the busiest international airport in Europe, handling aircraft and passengers of all the major airlines and home to the prestigious Imperial Airways whose fleet of modern airliners operated on routes trail-blazed by earlier pioneers to Europe, Africa, the Middle East and India.

With modern navigation and night flying aids, round the clock flying was possible except for one handicap, the predisposition of Croydon to become smog-bound. Quite often machines inbound to Croydon could be seen instead on the tarmac of Biggin Hill and Kenley when conditions caused them to divert.

The international crisis did not appear to affect Croydon very much although a token defence arrived consisting of one gunner subaltern, six men and one gun. When the crisis passed the airport became busier than ever, handling new and bigger machines, including the Lufthansa Fw Condor, the Imperial Airways' AW Ensigns and the beautiful DH Albatross, together with KLM and Swissair's Douglas DC3. Several RAF machines also visited. The atmosphere was friendly between the German and British staff at the airport and life continued normally until early August 1939, when increasing numbers of the Imperial Airways' long-haul fleet began to accumulate at Croydon and bookings for many overseas routes were not accepted. Contingency plans were drawn up for use in case of war and on 25th August, Flight Lieutenant Cooper, the adjutant of 615 Squadron at Kenley, arrived to take over as liaison officer if Croydon was taken over by the RAF.

On 27th August Sir Neville Henderson arrived back from a visit to

An Armstrong Whitworth Argosy in front of Croydon's famous control tower. (MAP)

Germany in a Lufthansa Ju 52 *Oswalde Boelke*, carrying Hitler's message to the British Government regarding Germany's rights over Poland. Returning also were passengers from Europe, holidaymakers and business people, who were clamouring for seats on aircraft but having to pay well over the odds. Croydon was busier than ever. On one day 1,500 people arrived, which was three times the normal amount.

On 30th August all flights were suspended and Croydon was taken over by the RAF as a satellite to Kenley, with Cooper appointed camp commandant. On the 31st the Air Ministry issued a prohibition on all private flying. The administration building was deserted and the once crowded booking hall with its airline counters and offices was now empty. The atmosphere was one of desolation, with old company brochures and literature scattered around. The staff had been evacuated back to their own countries to fight the war which now seemed inevitable. The buildings were later painted in camouflage designs and rope netting draped over the control tower.

Lufthansa had operated in and out of Croydon since the early days and it was felt by many that the frequent change of aircraft and crews had provided good training for German pilots and navigators in finding London by day and night. On occasion aircraft had wandered off course and flown over RAF Biggin Hill, usually to be greeted by a warning rocket fired by the duty pilot. Most of the staff had left by 31st

August when the last Lufthansa aircraft, the Ju 52 *Oswald Boelke*, left with any remaining personnel. With no fuss or emotion the aircraft taxied out, lined up on the south-east runway, awaited a green light from the tower and was away.

By 1st September Croydon no longer existed as a civil airport and the large Imperial Airways fleet of aircraft left for the comparative safety of Whitchurch, a small grass airfield near Bristol, where they became part of the National Air Communications organisation. In 1938 it had been felt that the best way to utilise the large civil fleet of aeroplanes in times of war was to use existing air transport companies under state charter. At Whitchurch the Imperial Airways and British Airways fleets together comprised 82 aircraft. The two companies were in any case to have merged to form a new company, the British Overseas Airways Corporation, in 1940 but when the war intervened amalgamation was brought forward for the state.

In 1939 the Air Navigation (Restriction in Time of War) Order prohibited all aircraft flying over eastern areas of England and Scotland. A line was drawn down the centre of England: to the east flying was controlled by Fighter Command and to the west several aerodromes were considered as safe for civil flying. With Croydon now an RAF station, any civilian flights in the south had to enter via

A Wellington DW1 after modification at Rollasons, Croydon, converted to create magnetic fields strong enough to detonate sea mines when the aircraft flew over them. (MAP)

615 Squadron arrive on 2nd September 1939 with their Gladiators, and airmen camp alongside their aircraft at dispersal. (LB of Sutton Heritage Service)

Shoreham airport. In the early days of the war, aircraft painted in the bright orange colour of neutral countries could often be seen parked on the ground at this airport on the Sussex coast.

The civilian industries at Croydon left the aerodrome, except for those engaged on war work such as Rollasons, who were overhauling engines and airframes. They were also modifying Wellington bombers, fitting huge degaussing rings which created magnetic fields sufficiently strong to explode magnetic sea mines when the aircraft flew over them.

On 2nd September, a bright sunny morning, the first of the RAF aircraft began to arrive. In flew 615 Squadron with its Gloster Gladiators from Kenley. Sixteen aircraft arrived in all, with twelve dispersed around the perimeter in the Forresters Drive area and the four reserve aircraft parked in the old Imperial Airways A hangar, which also served as a billet for the men. The ground crew of 615 were soon busy digging slit trenches, filling sandbags for machine gun posts, and erecting tents alongside their dispersal area. Later in the day the Hurricane Is of 17 Squadron swept in from North Weald followed by 1

615 Squadron's defensive machine gun post, 1939. (LB of Sutton Heritage Service)

Squadron Hurricanes from Biggin Hill. Croydon was now operating the three Kenley squadrons, two of which had moved out to allow the runways to be laid, but Kenley still retained overall control of operations. Croydon was host to over 50 fighters and a great number of personnel were housed in the hangars, with the officers in the Aerodrome Hotel.

At 11 am the following morning, Sunday 3rd September, the Prime Minister, Mr Neville Chamberlain spoke to the nation. A state of war now existed between Germany and the allies, Britain and France. A few minutes later, as if to reinforce this historic announcement the air raid sirens sounded, fortunately a false alarm as the general public stood a little bewildered, not knowing what to expect.

At Croydon there was a bustle of activity. No 3 Squadron had arrived on 2nd September, and now flew down to Manston in Kent each morning to escort Royal Navy ships which were minelaying around coastal waters. On 10th September, the first casualties of the war occurred when 3 Squadron, returning from Manston at dawn, ran

An Oerlikon cannon defensive emplacement (RAF No 2) in the playing fields alongside the airport and Purley Way. (LB of Sutton Heritage Service)

81

into low cloud and bad visibility, and a series of six crashes and forced landings took place.

A programme of night flying was introduced, no doubt to gain proficiency when used against the expected enemy night air raids. Croydon should have been the ideal aerodrome for night flying training, for as an international airport operating night flights it was equipped with the latest wireless, navigational aids and airfield lighting. The airfield could be floodlit with powerful Chance lights, it had a powerful Neon Pundit beacon visible for miles, and a Lorenz blind flying beam, together with the sodium street lights along the Purley Way. In wartime, however, lighting was restricted to Glim lamps or paraffin flares marking out the runway with only the occasional use of a Chance light.

The night flying was controlled from the tower by an officer, with the aircraft taxiing to the holding point signified by two orange Glim lamps. On receipt of a green light from the tower, the aircraft took off down the flare path of Glim lamps guided by a near-vertical white beam of light situated beyond the end of the runway which was switched off when the aircraft passed over it. Permission to land was by the usual green light from the tower, when the Chance light and the letter 'T' would be switched on immediately. A red light meant that permission to take off or land was refused.

Mishaps took place and on 8th September three Hurricanes returning from a night patrol were caught out by a heavy ground mist. The leader overshot the flarepath and, opening up the throttle to go around again, the engine stalled and the aircraft landed on the roof of the nurses' home of Purley Hospital. Fortunately, the pilot escaped with minor injuries. Other minor accidents followed and on 9th September 17 Squadron left for Debden. Night flying continued and 615 suffered two fatalities with one Gladiator crashing near Bletchingly and the other at Dorking, despite the switching on of the powerful Neon beacon to assist the pilot in finding the aerodrome.

In October things began to change. On the 10th, 145 Squadron was reformed at Croydon as a day and night fighter squadron with the twin-engined Bristol Blenheim Ifs. On the 12th, 3 Squadron left for temporary residence at Manston whilst the other squadrons prepared to fly out to France to join the British Expeditionary Force. On 13th November, 607 Squadron commanded by Squadron Leader Smith arrived with Gladiators to join 615 Squadron, commanded by Squadron Leader Harvey. Both squadrons flew to France on the 15th.

Accompanying the 32 Gladiators was a mixed fleet of old Imperial

The air armada prepares to move off for Merville in France, 15th November 1939.
Pictured are an ex-Imperial Airways Short L17, behind an ex-British Airways Fokker
XII; two Gladiators of 607 Squadron; and flying above, an Armstrong Whitworth
Ensign, ex-Imperial Airways. (LB of Sutton Heritage Service)

Airways aircraft, now with the NAC. Flying out from Croydon, they
carried spares, equipment and airmen. The types consisted of four
Armstrong Whitworth Ensigns, four De Havilland Rapides, two Short
17s named *Scylla* and *Syrinx*, one Miles Magister, one Avro 10 and one
Fokker Trimotor, the whole fleet landing an hour and a half later at a
very muddy Merville aerodrome, where all the cargo had to be offloaded by hand. 607 and 615 stayed at Merville until December when
they both moved to Vitry-en-Tardenois, with 615 sending a detachment
to St Inglevert. The assembly of such a huge fleet at Croydon delayed
the return of 3 Squadron from Manston until they had left for France.

Through the autumn months the new 145 Squadron under the
command of Squadron Leader J. D. Miller was acquiring its Blenheim
Ifs and pilots were converting to these machines at Hendon. They were
joined on 29th December by 92 Squadron, also recently reformed at
Tangmere, led by Squadron Leader R. Bushell and also flying the
Blenheim If. As the weather permitted, 92 and 145 were busy with
night flying exercises, mainly co-operating with AA batteries, calibrat-
ing searchlight and predictor gear, and early night fighter interception
practice.

Meanwhile, 3 Squadron was split into flights. A flight moved to

Ground crew clearing snow, January 1940, for a Bristol Blenheim I of 92 or 145 Squadron. (Imperial War Museum)

Hawkinge on 18th December, with B flight remaining at Croydon. Both carried out Channel patrols as the weather permitted, and on 29th January 1940, 3 Squadron moved back to its old home at Kenley, the first squadron to return after the improvements and laying of the runways.

The night flying operations for 92 and 145 in the new year were both frustrating and hazardous. Engine trouble plagued the Blenheims and damage to the rear fuselage by heavy landings on the frozen ground was common. The de-icing of aircraft dispersed outside was difficult and time consuming and even when the weather was favourable, quite often only two or three machines were serviceable.

There were many incidents. Machines caught out in bad weather were having to divert, a collision took place between two Blenheims, a forced landing followed engine failure at Wallington and on 24th February came a most tragic accident.

A Blenheim of 92 Squadron, piloted by Pilot Officer R. Whitmarsh, was on circuit training when, after an hour's dual instruction, he was sent solo. The Blenheim took off but failed to gain height and crashed on to houses in Forresters Drive near to the western boundary of the airfield. No 45 Forresters Drive was demolished and caught fire; the pilot and a young woman and her small daughter were tragically killed. The following enquiry noted that on this evening the lighting was inadequate and highlighted the unsuitability of Croydon for operational training, recommending that it should revert to satellite status now that Kenley and Biggin Hill had runways laid. The Battle of Britain delayed that decision but afterwards Redhill was selected in preference to Croydon for training and operating night fighters.

The very bad winter of 1940 also affected Whitchurch aerodrome where part of the NAC fleet, including several pre-war Croydon stalwarts, were parked. On the night of 19th March, a sudden and severe gale struck, sweeping the airfield where a variety of aeroplanes were parked including two of the old Croydon-based Imperial Airways HP42s, *Heracles* and *Hanno*. Before the ground crew could reach them the force of the wind under the large biplane wings tore the holding-down pegs out of the ground and despite efforts to start the engines, the wind lifted the big machines and threw them backwards into a field behind, wrecking both beyond repair. None of the remaining fleet of HP42s was to survive 1940, either by accident or enemy action.

In March the Blenheims at Croydon were retired. 92 Squadron received their Spitfire Is and a Miles Master, a dual conversion trainer, and 145 Squadron their Hurricane Is. In the following weeks the airport was busy with conversion training programmes but not without mishap! This continued into the first week of May when on the 7th, 145 left for Filton and on the 8th, 92 left for Northolt.

On 10th May 1940 came the shock news that the Germans were bombing Holland and Belgium and attacking France. The 'Phoney War' was over and the German Panzers were racing across France and the Netherlands to be stopped only by the Channel.

In France, 607 and 615 Squadrons which had flown out from Croydon in November, were soon engaged in heavy fighting, trying to stem the German advance. They had moved to Abbeville in April, with 615 converting to Hurricanes, and both had spent their time mainly in quiet Channel patrols. Now they were engaged in heavy fighting, escorting Blenheims attacking ground targets and making low level attacks on advancing troops. Their losses were high and by the 20th, 615 had to revert to Gladiators for airfield defence. On the 10th, 145 flew out from Filton to join them with fresh Hurricanes, answering the call to send more fighter squadrons. On 20th May, due to the ferocity of the German advance, their airfields became untenable. 607 flew from

The Lysander was the workhorse of the Army Co-operation squadrons. 2 Squadron flew in to Croydon for a brief stay on return from France, 20th May 1940. (MAP)

Béthune back to Croydon and 615 flew back from Abbeville and Le Touquet, nine aircraft escorting transports to Kenley and three to Croydon for repairs at Rollasons.

The airport had been left empty after 145 and 92 Squadrons left earlier in the month but by 20th May damaged aircraft were flying in from squadrons in France for repairs. There also arrived a Canadian sergeant and 27 men of 110 Squadron RCAF from the School of Army Flying, Old Sarum. They were a servicing vanguard for 2 Squadron, who were expected to arrive from France with their Lysanders. Thirteen Lysanders and a Leopard Moth actually arrived later in the day but their stay was short as they left for Bekesbourne the next day along with their servicing party.

On the 21st, both 607 and 615 Squadrons' ground crews embarked at Boulogne for Dover and then to Tidworth where the billeting, they found, was excellent. Next day 607's crews left for Croydon by train and 615's for Kenley, but with Kenley full, 615 were diverted to Croydon as well and were finally billeted in an unused girls' school.

Two days later, on the 23rd, Croydon became the receiving station for large fleets of transport aircraft of the National Air Communications which arrived from France all day carrying troops, some very badly injured. Croydon had never handled so many aircraft in a 24 hour period. After the offloading of personnel and the wounded into waiting ambulances, the aircraft were flown out for dispersal at Hendon and Heston.

In contrast to the evacuating aircraft arriving, a major air lift of tinned food by a mixed fleet of 33 aircraft had been mounted on the 22nd May. Twenty two tons of iron rations were transported to Merville, eight miles to the north of Béthune, for troops still fighting in France. The operation was ended by enemy action. One AW Ensign BOAC *Elysian* was destroyed on the ground at Merville by attacking Me 109s and two Savoia-Marchettis and a Douglas DC3 were missing. Another Ensign BOAC *Euralyus* was attacked over the Channel and badly damaged, crashlanding at Lympne. The old Imperial Airways fleet was gradually being destroyed or lost and with the overrun of France, another Ensign *Ettrick*, stranded at Le Bourget, was captured by the Germans.

The evacuation of the BEF at Dunkirk continued until 4th June 1940 and 607 Squadron, resting after their return from France, left for Usworth with some of the ground crew travelling in one of the remaining Ensigns. They were replaced by 111 Squadron from North Weald, commanded by Squadron Leader J. Thompson.

Without bases in France, 111 Squadron flew daily patrols with 615 from Kenley and sometimes with other squadrons. At this time, squadrons could still land at a safe airfield in French territory not yet occupied, to refuel and rearm. On 8th June 111, on patrol with 615 in the Le Tréport area, landed at Dreux and did just this without trouble. On the 9th, they patrolled in the Le Tréport-Aumale-Poix area and noted that the city of Rouen was in flames. On the 11th, with further patrols in the Fécamp-Le Tréport area, enemy aircraft were encountered. In the dogfight one Me 109 was damaged and another Me 109 and a Ju 87 were listed as probables. Patrols continued until the fall of France.

On 21st June, 501 Squadron arrived from Jersey where they had been covering the evacuation of the remaining BEF from Cherbourg after the fall of France. The aircraft were repaired, the airmen re-kitted and granted a few days' leave. The squadron flew a few patrols at the end of the month before leaving with their Hurricanes on 3rd July for Middle Wallop.

The Luftwaffe now had forward bases on the Channel coast and were engaged on probing missions, beginning with small raids on English coastal towns and Channel shipping. With the intensity of the air fighting increasing by mid June, 111's score stood at 47 enemy aircraft destroyed with 14 probables. On the 21st, they acted as escort to 801 Squadron of the Fleet Air Arm, whose Blackburn Skuas and Rocs dive-bombed gun emplacements south-west of Calais. On the 27th, they escorted Blenheims on a photo-reconnaissance mission and on the 30th, went again to Merville to photograph the airfield, when enemy aircraft were encountered and four Blenheims were lost.

On the ground the defences at Croydon were strengthened after the Prime Minister had warned of the threat of imminent invasion.

The 4th July 1940 saw the first Canadians at Croydon when 1 Squadron RCAF arrived, followed by their Hurricanes. Canadian-built to an earlier specification and shipped to England, the aircraft were fitted with wooden two-bladed propellers but during their stay at Croydon they were eventually uprated with the three-bladed metal propellers. They were commanded by Squadron Leader E. McNabb and during their stay were brought up to active service readiness under the watchful eye of the battle-hardened 111 Squadron.

On 10th July, now regarded as the opening day of the Battle of Britain, the fighting over the Channel intensified and 111 were scrambled from Croydon to intercept a raid by Dornier 17s on a convoy off Folkestone. A furious scrap ensued. Pilot Officer T. Higgs claimed a Dornier but was then seen to collide with another, his Hurricane falling away and the pilot baling out. Despite searches by the rescue launch he could not be found.

On 19th July, 111 flew down to Hawkinge early in the morning and were put on standby. Just after noon bombs began to fall on Folkestone and nine Boulton Paul Defiants of 141 'Cock' Squadron were scrambled from Hawkinge to intercept the raid. Ordered to climb to Dungeness, they were attacked by 20 Me 109fs of II/JG2, the famous Richtofen Geschwader.

Up to now the Defiant had achieved quite a success in air fighting but it was widely felt this was probably due to them being mistaken for Hurricanes, as when attacked from the side or rear the attackers were unexpectedly met with the fire of the four machine guns in the rear turret. The Defiant had no forward firing armament and was actually very vulnerable when attacked from the front or underneath. This was soon realised by the Messerschmitt pilots and this particular attack was made by diving under the formation of Defiants, climbing up and attacking the underside. The result was devastating, every aircraft was hit. Two immediately fell in flames whilst the others jockeyed for position so that their gunners could aim. Meanwhile, 111 had been scrambled from Hawkinge and arrived to join in the fight. Pilot Officer

Messerschmitt Me 110 long range fighter/bomber. (MAP)

Simpson claimed one Me 109 and the squadron four more. Sergeant Powell of 141 Squadron also claimed one Me 109, but of the nine Defiants that left Hawkinge seven were lost.

The Channel attacks continued throughout July. Hitler's plan to draw the RAF into battle and destroy it was unsuccessful and by the end of July he realised that the present tactics were not working and instructed that the raids should intensify and move inland to attack airfields, communication systems and radar.

August saw a further increase in Channel activity and by the 12th the raids had moved inland, with the coastal radar stations being attacked by the fighter-bomber group Erprobungsgruppe 210 led by the Me 110 specialist, Hauptmann Walter Rubensdörffer. In the following days the airfields of Lympne, Manston, Detling, Eastchurch and Middle Wallop were badly damaged by enemy raiders including Erpro 210, whose luck seemed to be running with them.

August 15th was another brilliant day of that hot summer. The Luftwaffe sent the largest number of raids so far against airfields and radar stations from the north of England to Weymouth in the south, from airfields based from Norway to France. In the afternoon the raids switched to targets in 11 Group in the south-east and by 3 pm, 111 Squadron were in action over Dover in a head-on attack against a formation of Dornier 215s. Three enemy aircraft were destroyed with three probables but 111 Squadron had three aircraft damaged. Squadron Leader E. McNab, the commanding officer of 1 Squadron RCAF who were staying at Croydon, flew on this occasion with 111 and scored the squadron's first victory by shooting down a Dornier. Refuelled and rearmed, 111 with three aircraft short had their second interception over Thorney Island against Ju 88s and Me 110s. One Ju 88 and one Me 110 were destroyed but 111 Squadron lost one pilot and another was wounded. Attacks had been widespread on the towns of Portsmouth, Weymouth and Portland and the airfields of Lympne and Hawkinge.

The third wave of over 70 planes was plotted at 6.15 pm, but soon broken up by intercepting squadrons. Amongst the raiders was, once again, the fighter-bomber unit Erpro 210, led by Hauptmann Rubens-dörffer and heading at low level into the Biggin Hill, Kenley and Croydon area. At 6.50 pm, nine Hurricanes of 111 Squadron were scrambled from Croydon and waited at 10,000 feet over London for the raiders to show.

On the ground it was a fine summer's evening with a slight heat haze. Just before 7 pm the Me 110s and Me 109s of Erpro 210 dived onto a seemingly undefended and unsuspecting Croydon, but just before the first bombs were loosed at 6.59 pm, the nine Hurricanes of 111 Squadron were down amongst them. Many of the bombs consequently fell wide of the target, with several outside the aerodrome causing great damage.

The commanding officer, Squadron Leader Thompson, claimed the first Me 110, which crashlanded in a field. He then chased and downed an Me 109 along the Purley Way. By this time the Hurricanes of 32 Squadron had joined from Biggin Hill and a furious scrap ensued. The ground defences of machine guns and Oerlikon cannon had opened up, adding to the noise and confusion of the gunfire and bombs exploding. The Me 109s were the first to go, their fuel running low, leaving the Me 110s to form a defensive circle and fend for themselves. Sergeants Dymond and Craig of 111 Squadron both claimed an Me 110 and another was shared by Flight Lieutenant Connors and Sergeant T. Wallace. The Hurricanes of 32 Squadron claimed two others. As the remaining Me 110s sped for home, Squadron Leader Thompson followed one to Rotherfield in Sussex. With a final burst from his guns the Me 110 of the leader, Hauptmann Rubensdörffer, reared up and crashed near Bletchinglye Farm, exploding and killing him and his gunner, Obergefreiter Kretzer.

The Croydon log reports that the raid by 25 to 30 Me 110s, Heinkel

The British NSF factory alongside Croydon airport, completely destroyed in the air raid of 15th August 1940. (LB of Sutton Heritage Service)

113s and Me 109s lasted five or ten minutes and began before the air raid sirens were sounded. Civilians were caught unawares in the streets, going home from work, or having their evening meal. This was the heaviest and most damaging raid of the day and on the airfield, the southern wing of the terminal block was damaged by an armour piercing high explosive bomb and by incendiaries. The control tower was machine-gunned and damaged by fire. The armoury received a direct hit and was burnt out. The windows of A hangar were damaged, D hangar was also badly damaged and C hangar, previously used by Rollasons, received a direct hit with many of the aircraft inside destroyed. There was also damage to the officers' mess, the shelter trenches, and the MT petrol store. The airfield itself was pockmarked with bomb craters.

The damage caused outside the aerodrome to the civilian buildings and population was severe and the ferocity and surprise of the attack left many people deeply shocked. The British NSF factory, making electrical components for the RAF, received direct hits and was completely destroyed, killing over 30 people. The nearby Bourjois soap and perfume factory received a direct hit on the soap department, killing five workmen. Scores of houses, and a bus, were damaged. The total number of casualties is open to question but the official number is given as 62 killed, with 37 seriously injured. The total number of bombs recorded was seven 500 lb HE, two medium HE and many incendiaries.

The Dornier 17 of Hauptmann Joachim Roth, shot down after the attack on Kenley on 18th August 1940. (Imperial War Museum)

For the Luftwaffe, 15th August had seen the greatest number of sorties flown against England in a day and their greatest number of losses. It became known to them as Black Thursday. The official figure was 75 fighters and bombers destroyed, with many high ranking Luftwaffe commanders killed; the RAF lost 30 fighters and 13 pilots. This day also saw the first raid into the London area, forbidden by Hitler, which raises the question of whether the raid on Croydon was a mistake — was the airfield thought to be Kenley?

By the next day the bomb-cratered grass airfield had been repaired. 1 Squadron RCAF, modifications complete and painted in camouflage colours, left for Northolt to become operational as No 401 in the Dominion 400 series. 111 Squadron was operational by midday and ordered to Hawkinge, but diverted to Dungeness to intercept 200 Dorniers and their Me 109 escorts. In a head-on attack one Hurricane piloted by Flight Lieutenant Ferris collided with the lead Dornier, the Hurricane crashing at Marden and the Dornier at Brenchley. Squadron Leader Thompson shot down a Dornier at Tonbridge and Sergeant Cray destroyed another over Tunbridge Wells. Pilot Officer J. Walker claimed an Me 109 and Sergeant Wallace downed one Me 109 after being jumped by six of them.

On the 18th it was the turn of Biggin Hill and Kenley, when they faced a three-pronged attack by two waves of Dornier 17s and Junkers 88s, followed by the low-flying attack of the nine Dornier 17s of the 9th Staffel, JG76 led by Hauptman Roth (see Kenley). Just before 1 pm Kenley performed a survival scramble of 64 and 615 Squadrons and at Croydon the controller scrambled 111 to patrol Kenley at 3,000 feet when the raiders' intentions became clear. However, the co-ordination of the raid had gone wrong, the high-flying raiders were late and the low-level attack had no alternative but to proceed without them. As the bombs began to fall, 111 Squadron spotted the fleeing raiders below and dived to the attack behind them.

The lead Hurricane of Flight Lieutenant S. Connors sped in over the battle below but before he could engage, his Hurricane was hit and fell in flames, killing him. His number two, Flight Officer Simpson, latched on to another hedge-hopping Dornier, getting in several bursts, but his closing speed was too high and seeing that one of the Dornier's engines was on fire, he turned away to avoid a collision. As he did so he exposed the underside of the Hurricane and was hit by return fire, forcing him to put down on the golf course at Woodcote Park. The lead Dornier of Hauptman Roth, on fire, was chased by Sergeants Dymond and Brown, who continued raking it with machine gun fire until the pilot, Oberleutnant Lamberty, put it down with a splintering crash in a field at Leaves Green.

Sergeant Harry Newton became separated from the rest of the squadron at 3,000 feet, spotted a Dornier below and closed for the attack. Firing off one burst, his Hurricane was hit by return fire. Too low to bale out, he climbed the blazing Hurricane until the engine stopped and then parachuted down, to land at Tatsfield only 50 yards from the wreck of his blazing Hurricane. 111 Squadron continued the chase until fuel and ammunition ran out.

The high level raid was broken up over Kenley and some of the Dornier 17s and Junkers 88s diverted their attention to West Malling aerodrome, with five aircraft heading for Croydon. The attack lasted only five minutes but included eleven high explosive bombs and many incendiaries, damaging A hangar and destroying one aircraft of 111 Squadron and damaging another.

On 19th August a weary and battle-scarred 111 Squadron left for Debden for a well earned rest, to be replaced by the Hurricanes of 85 Squadron led by Squadron Leader Peter Townsend. They were

Messerschmitt Me 109, the front line fighter of the Luftwaffe during the Battle of Britain. The aircraft pictured belonged to top scoring Major Adolf Galland. (MAP)

dispersed on the western side of the airfield and the officers and men were billeted in requisitioned houses in nearby Forresters Drive. Their arrival coincided with five days of bad weather and gave the squadron a well earned respite, but this was suddenly broken in the small hours of the 24th by the deafening sound of bombs exploding at 85's dispersal point, destroying two Hurricanes. The bombs had been dropped by a lone raider circling in the darkness above and others fell outside the airfield. One hit the Bourjois factory and for days the air was scented with perfume.

The weather was clearing by now and the Duke of Kent was expected at the airfield for a visit at ten o'clock that morning. Squadron Leader Townsend had been on his way to the bathroom with his sponge bag when the alarm went and within minutes he was airborne with six Hurricanes on their way to engage 100-plus enemy planes over Dover. One Me 109 was shot down by Sergeant S. Allard, his best pilot. Back at Croydon the Duke was waiting for their return and on landing, Townsend was quickly asked to line up the squadron for inspection. Whilst introducing the pilots of 85 a quick glance at his left tunic pocket revealed a toothbrush sticking out, taken into battle from the interrupted ablutions!

Squadron Leader Peter Townsend, DFC, with pilots of 85 Squadron. (Imperial War Museum)

On the 26th, 85 Squadron were airborne in the afternoon to meet a diversionary attack over Kent. Twelve Dornier 17s of 7/KG3 were acting as decoys, with a top cover escort of Me 109s from JG3 and JG54. 85's Hurricanes, throttling back slightly, made a head-on attack on the Dorniers, firing until the last moment, then with sticks down hard, feeling the negative 'g', they were under the bombers to avoid the fighters. Three Dorniers were trailing smoke and crashlanded and one other failed to return to Melville. One Hurricane of 85 was lost but the pilot parachuted to safety.

By now the Luftwaffe were bombing by night and some pilots from day squadrons who were qualified as night operational, flew night patrols. 85 had some night flyers and Squadron Leader Townsend later described taking off from Croydon at night on 28th August with only goose-neck paraffin flares lighting the runway, flying two unsuccessful patrols and being back on the ground by 3 am ready to fly four patrols during the coming day.

In the morning patrol, 85 Squadron intercepted 20 Me 109s over Dungeness, claiming six, two to Pilot Officer Sam Allard, 85's top scorer. On the third patrol at 4 pm, 85 joined 253 from Kenley led by Squadron Leader Tom Gleave and, climbing above Beachy Head, spotted 18 Heinkels, decoys for about 200 Me 109s above them. Aiming for the bombers, they were attacked by the Me 109s diving from above. Squadron Leader Townsend caught an Me 109 in the turn and sent it into the sea off Hastings, and Flight Lieutenant Hamilton claimed another; two young pilots of 85 were shot down but happily baled out safely. Then it was back to Croydon, to refuel and rearm in five minutes and scramble again at 6.15 pm.

The 30th saw the beginning of the fiercest 48 hours of fighting so far, an all out effort by the Luftwaffe to destroy the airfields. 85 saw action in the morning, breaking up a formation of Heinkels and Me 110s. Six Me 110s were destroyed and two Heinkels by Sam Allard.

On 31st August 1940, 85 were scrambled during lunch from Croydon as bombs began to fall on the airfield. To the east black smoke was seen rising from a coinciding attack on Biggin Hill. The first bombs fell on Croydon at 12.55 pm from twelve raiding aircraft and the attack lasted six minutes, damaging a vacant hangar used by Redwing Aircraft and shelters nearby. In the air Townsend, furious that his airfield was being attacked again, was soon in the thick of it. The Me 110s had formed the usual defensive circle but he hit an Me 109 in a climbing turn. Rolling his aircraft over, another Me 110 was lined up but before he could open fire his Hurricane was badly hit. Baling out, he landed in a back garden near Hawkhurst and was now conscious of a severe pain in his left foot. Assisted by a policeman, he was taken to Hawkhurst Hospital and then to Croydon General Hospital where the nose cone of a cannon shell was removed from his left foot along with his big toe which was amputated.

85 Squadron, now commanded by Sam Allard, continued at Croydon and were joined on 1st September by 72 Squadron's Spitfires commanded by Squadron Leader A. Collins. Soon in action against constant attacks, their losses mounted. On the 2nd, the remnants of 85 left for Castle Camps and 111 Squadron returned from Debden.

On 7th September 1940 the raids suddenly switched from the airfields to London and in the afternoon three large formations of bombers with fighter escorts flew over Croydon heading for London's East End and Dockland. 111 had been patrolling Maidstone and returned to Croydon to find Me 109s waiting overhead. They immediately tore into them, sending them packing, 111 suffering one casualty. The next day 111 flew to Drem in Scotland and 605 'County of Warwick' Squadron flew in from Drem, commanded by Squadron Leader W. Churchill. They met a scene unfamiliar to them – the sight of London burning beneath huge palls of smoke.

Night raids now commenced in earnest and the Blitz continued well into 1941. On the 8th, 605 Squadron saw their first action. Flying with

253 from Kenley they attacked a formation of Ju 88s and Do 215s over the Maidstone-Tunbridge Wells area, turning them back. They were attacked by the Me 109 escort but one Me 109 was destroyed and five damaged for the loss of one aircraft, the pilot safely baling out. The next day, Flight Lieutenant Archie McKellar claimed four aircraft in one sortie. Scrambled to intercept Heinkels at 20,000 feet with an Me 109 escort above, McKellar's section made a head-on attack with the sun behind them. With a perfect target, a vic of three, he opened fire at the lead Heinkel which exploded violently, bringing down the other aircraft either side. An Me 109 was downed on the way home.

On the 14th, 72 Squadron returned to Biggin Hill after two weeks of heavy fighting. They had destroyed twelve enemy aircraft but had lost two aircraft with several damaged and Squadron Leader Collins had been seriously injured.

605 Squadron often flew with 253 and 501 from Kenley as a Hurricane Wing and on 15th September were in action from late morning until early evening against the Luftwaffe's 'one last great effort'. It was a beautiful autumn day and by 11 am the enemy were massing over the Pas de Calais as Air Vice Marshal Park scrambled his 23 fighter squadrons. Kenley's 253 and 501 were airborne at 11.15 am, with 605 following at 11.40 am and immediately engaging a fleet of Dorniers and Heinkels in a running battle over Kent and Surrey. In one engagement Pilot Officer M. Cooper-Slipper, flying No 2 to the section leader, encountered a vic of bombers from above and his Hurricane was hit. Losing control, he collided with a Heinkel. The Hurricane, now minus a wing, went into an inverted spin, the effect of which was to eject him when the hood was opened, to parachute safely into a hop garden. Greeted with suspicion by the hop pickers at first, he was soon being entertained in the local hostelry before returning to Croydon.

The battle raged all day with such a sustained effort and heavy bombing that it was thought an invasion was imminent. The Forces were put on invasion alert. September 15th was a critical day in the Battle of Britain, when the whole might of the Luftwaffe was met by 'the few'. But the defences held – so much so that Hitler postponed the invasion of England indefinitely.

The day raids continued gradually tailing off as winter approached, changing in style as the heavy bombers gave way to the more diverse raids by the fighter-bombers, Me 109s and Me 110s carrying one or two 500 lb bombs. 605 were kept busy dealing with these fast, high flying aircraft which changed into highly effective fighters once they had discharged their bombs.

The night attacks on London continued without let up, the raiding aircraft flying continuously over Croydon aerodrome. In September it received two attacks. On the night of 11th September there were intermittent attacks not causing any significant damage, but on the 23rd/24th, nine incendiaries fell along Stafford Road, damaging the old Redwing hangar roof. The hangar was housing F company of the 12th Queen's Royal Regiment, the guard at the aerodrome at the time, but luckily no one was injured.

In October 1940 there were further raids around the airfield on the 15th and 19th, and on the 24th a stick of five HE bombs fell in the north-west corner.

When 111 Squadron left in September, 605 remained in sole charge at Croydon through the rest of the Battle and afterwards. On 21st October, during a fighter-bomber raid, their leader Archie McKellar shot down an Me 109, bringing his score to 21 destroyed, three probables and three damaged. During his time at Croydon he was awarded the DSO, DFC and Bar but sadly was killed when his Hurricane crashed two days later. 605 stayed at Croydon until 25th February 1941 when they left for Martlesham and were replaced by 17 Squadron with their Hurricanes.

By now the RAF were on the offensive and 17 stayed a month, taking part in the early fighter sweeps with the Kenley Wing until 7th April when 1 Squadron arrived with their Hurricanes from Kenley. The squadron had several Czech pilots and on the morning of their arrival, four Hurricanes of B flight led by Pilot Officer Robinson with three Czech sergeants patrolled Mayfield. Over Dungeness at 25,000 feet they were vectored to Cap Gris Nez where they encountered three Bf 109s in a wide vic formation. One Hurricane had returned with engine trouble but the remaining three engaged in a furious scrap with the yellow-nosed Messerschmitts. Sergeant Kuttelwascher noticed a Bf 109 below and dived to the attack, hitting its wing root with two short bursts. White smoke came from the machine as it went into a dive and crashed into a wood below.

On 1st May 1941, 1 Squadron moved to the more southerly airfield of Redhill and became part of the Kenley Hurricane Wing. Redhill was now becoming the favoured satellite of Kenley for the forthcoming offensive operations, whereas Croydon's role was changing from fighter operations to one of army co-operation.

On 25th May, No 11 Group Flight, Army Co-operation Unit (later 287 Squadron) was formed at Heston under the leadership of Flight Lieutenant R. Smith and on 5th June authority was given for the move to Croydon. The next day, four long-nosed Blenheim IVs and six Lysander IIIs were flown to Croydon and the vacated billets in Forresters Drive were taken over, with No 27 as the HQ. Things got off to a bad start when a Lysander flying in to join them crashed on landing. Croydon was established as the home base and No 11 AACU operated with detachments at many other airfields, assisting the AA units in their areas. The first detachments were at Tangmere, Hornchurch and Merston, returning home for servicing etc. Croydon kept about 70 ground and maintenance staff but only four pilots and crew with their aircraft, the rest being on detachment.

The Lysanders were employed for target drogue towing whilst the Blenheims were busy with AA batteries and Home Guard exercises, plus at night AA calibration, D/F homing exercises and searchlight calibration. Kenley control had been instrumental in using radar-assisted searchlights to find the height and track of a target, and using this information to guide night fighters to within the limited range of their Airborne Interception radar sets. The squadron were kept busy and by September were flying about 600 hours a month.

On 12th August 1941 a new Canadian squadron, 414 (Army Co-operation), was formed at Croydon under Squadron Leader G. G. Elms from eight officers and 69 men from 400 Squadron based at Odiham. The squadron was dispersed in the Plough Lane area and took over houses there – No 9 as HQ and No 11 as the photographic section.

In the next month the squadron was busy picking up its aircraft, two Lysander IIIs on loan and seven American Curtiss P40 Tomahawk I fighters from Eastleigh and Colherne. The Lysander was not proving successful in the latest army co-operation work and its slow speed made it vulnerable to enemy fighter attacks. Several replacement aircraft were tried and the Tomahawk was selected as the replacement on availability, as all Spitfires and Hurricanes were going to fighter squadrons. Fitted with the 1,090 hp Allison V-12 engine it had a top speed of 328 mph and, armed with six machine guns, it was quite a rugged performer but its performance was not up to the Hurricane or Spitfire. In September some Tomahawk IIs arrived and in the next months the squadron was concerned with working up to operational standard. On 2nd October the Duke of Kent visited Croydon to inspect the squadron and watch a display of formation flying.

Intensive gunnery exercises were carried out at Weston Zoyland in Somerset with the Lysanders towing drogues and the Tomahawks firing off some 22,000 rounds. Photographic exercises, included practising the technique of taking mosaic and oblique pictures.

A Mustang I of 414 Squadron up from Croydon, 1942. (P. McCue)

287 Squadron continued its AA co-operation duties and tried out many new types of aircraft appearing suitable for this kind of work. By December they had on charge five Blenheim IVs, nine Lysanders, three Hurricanes, four Lockheed Hudsons and five Miles Master IIIs, with detachments at Debden, Hornchurch, Merston, Heston and Martlesham. Heavy circuit training took place with the new types and in the new year more searchlight and Ground Controlled Interception exercises were carried out to further night fighter operations. A new GCI radar station at Pevensey was operating taking plots from the main sector operation centre. They were using the seaward facing radar, and this new information together with their own radar enabled them to direct the fighters on to the raiders until the enemy came within the scope of their AI radar sets.

In June 1942 the superb North American P51 Mustang I fighter/ attack aircraft began arriving to replace the Tomahawks of 414 and other squadrons. Fitted with an Allison V-12 engine, 1,150 hp, it was capable of a top speed of 390 mph and, with an armament of eight machine guns, it was on a par with the latest marks of Spitfires. It had a much greater range than the Hurricane or Spitfire and was admirably suited to the low and medium altitude work performed by the army co-operation and fighter reconnaissance squadrons. Engine performance fell away rapidly above 15,000 feet but low down, the Mustang was outstanding.

On 1st July two Polish squadrons, 302 and 317, arrived at Croydon for offensive operations with their Spitfire Vbs. Their arrival in bad weather was heralded by five landing incidents, including one Spitfire bursting a tyre and pulling up just short of Air Marshal Sir A. Barratt who was visiting! One other Polish and two Czech squadrons with servicing echelons arrived at Redhill on the same day; Croydon and Redhill were now acting as forward bases for a secret operation.

Bad weather held up operations until 8th July 1942 when the squadrons were brought to readiness. On the 12th there were two operations, one a feint Rodeo to Mardyke and the other to escort Circus No 198, with the Tangmere Wing, but no enemy aircraft were sighted.

On the 13th, a Rodeo to Abbeville aerodrome took place but no enemy aircraft were flushed out. The second sweep was to escort Bostons on Circus No 199 in bombing Boulogne railway station. On the way home the squadron went to assist the Biggin Hill Wing, under attack near Le Touquet. Happily, all aircraft returned safely. The operations continued until the end of the month when the squadrons returned to their home airfields. They had been assembled to participate in the Dieppe landings but this was postponed until August.

Earlier, in the new year of 1942, a new detachment of 287 had been formed at Fairlop and later one at Biggin Hill with Miles Master IIIs. In May and June, 20 Boulton Paul Defiants and four Airspeed Oxfords had been put on charge at Croydon and a great deal of night flying took place on GCI practice using searchlights as beacons.

On the night of 27th July a Defiant flown by Flying Officer Russel was on an exercise flying 'boxes' (rectangular patrol sectors codenamed red, blue and amber) at 9,000 feet when they were vectored on to a Junkers 88 in amber sector. The aircraft was quickly located and Russel manoeuvred the Defiant to allow the four machine guns in the rear turret to be aimed by the gunner. One short burst at 150 yards and closing, then another three-second burst at 75 yards caused an explosion in the Junkers' cockpit. The aircraft dived steeply into the haze and contact was lost. No help was given by the searchlights and the aircraft was claimed as a probable.

By July detachments were at Ford, Debden, Ipswich and Hunsden and the squadron had flown over 1,000 hours, 537 of them at Croydon. There were also some new arrivals at Croydon, when 116 with some Oxfords and Ansons on radar calibration joined 287, 414 and No 1 Delivery Flight who were operating DH Dominies.

On 30th June, 414 had flown their first operational mission, when three Mustangs flew a defensive patrol along the south coast. By July they were fully operational and were engaged with the Canadian army, low flying and observing artillery shoots at Sennybridge in Wales. This was to gain experience for when the Allies returned to Europe, when they would be artillery spotting. In early August they took part in Operation Dryshod, an invasion exercise at Abbotsinch, working up for a coming operation. By the 15th the squadron log indicates that they were getting impatient to put their training into action.

There wasn't long to wait, for on the 17th the squadron was put on standby and on the 18th pilots were engaged on Operation Jubilee, the Dieppe landings. On 19th August, 414 flew nine two-plane sorties in good weather on tactical reconnaissance along the French coast and encountered heavy flak. Two aircraft were hit but the pilots were safe: Flight Lieutenant Clarke was hit by an attack from an Fw 190 over Dieppe and ditched in the sea suffering slight injuries, while Flying Officer McQuade was hit by flak and abandoned the sortie. Pilot Officer Stow was jumped by an Fw 190 at low altitude and, taking violent evasive action, hit a telegraph pole, losing three feet of the starboard wing but making it home.

The Mustang I was considered inferior to the Fw 190 in performance but Flying Officer Hill in his second mission over Dieppe was jumped by three Fw 190s and credited with destroying one, believed to be the first by a Mustang. On 20th August, Air Marshal Barratt visited the squadron and congratulated them on their first successful operation.

There were more practice attacks at Weston Zoyland and a dummy attack on 'parachutists' at Ditchling Beacon, but on 1st November 1942 came a change in the style of sorties flown when a combined operation was attempted with the Tangmere Wing carrying out a Popular and Rodeo operation. Further exercises were carried out with the Canadian Army, including air/ground signalling with a beacon lamp, and on 2nd December the squadron, now 414 Fighter Reconnaissance, moved to the new airfield at Dunsfold in Surrey.

116 and 287 Squadrons continued their role as army co-operation squadrons, but in 1943 Croydon airfield started to revert to some of its peacetime activities with the arrival of No 110 Wing, Transport

Command equipped with Douglas Dakotas and the return of BOAC, which after the successful invasion of Europe on 6th June 1944 started scheduled services in November. In July 1944, 116 and 287 Squadrons moved out, leaving the airport almost back to its peacetime role.

By the end of the war 110 Wing had carried over 100,000 passengers and the smaller independents such as Railway Air Services, Jersey Airways and Morton Air Services were moving back.

A few Dakota squadrons – 271, 147 and 435 RCAF – used Croydon airport until 1946 when it reverted to full peacetime flying, but when Heathrow was officially named as the London Airport its future was sealed as an international airport. Its size and location precluded the use of the newer breed of aircraft. British European Airways, set up from the services inaugurated by No 110 Wing, left for Gatwick, leaving behind the independents and some flying clubs which continued flying until 1959 when the airport closed for good.

Parts of the flying field remain and the occasional air show is held but most of the aerodrome is now built on as industrial premises and the Roudshaw Estate. The famous control tower and aerodrome hotel remain, however, as living monuments to a golden bygone age of aviation and Croydon's stirring history is preserved in the archives of the London Borough of Sutton Heritage Service and a vigorous Croydon Airport Society.

5
KENLEY

In 1936, as part of the modernisation and reorganisation programme, the RAF was split into its functional parts and Kenley, the only RAF aerodrome in the county, became part of the newly formed Fighter Command under Air Marshal Hugh Dowding. It formed part of a ring of similar Fighter Command airfields around the capital responsible for its defence.

Dowding considered the main threat to Great Britain would be from German bombers operating from European bases and initially established two defence groups based on the known bombers' range. No 10 Group was to cover the North and Midlands, and No 11 Group to cover the South. Each Group was subdivided into sectors and Kenley, part of No 11 Group, was given control of Sector B ranging from Virginia Water in the north to a line crossing the coast at Middleton, and also from Petersham to Bexhill encompassing the airfields of Croydon, Gatwick, Redhill and Friston.

At the time of the reorganisation the war in Abyssinia and concern about the growth of the German military machine produced great apprehension for the future and thoughts turned to defence. The halcyon days of peace-time flying gave way to training on the new fighter types coming into service. In 1936 Kenley had two squadrons in residence, 3 and 17, both equipped with Bristol Bulldog biplane fighters, though 3 were temporarily overseas keeping an eye on the Abyssinian crisis. August 1936 saw the Bulldogs of 17 Squadron replaced by Gloster Gauntlets and 3 Squadron, on return from overseas in March 1937, received the new Gloster Gladiator, the ultimate in biplane fighter design. It was a beautiful machine well loved by pilots, capable of 250 mph and with four machine guns, but already outdated by the new generation of high speed monopolane fighters being developed in Britain as well as by Messerschmitt in Germany.

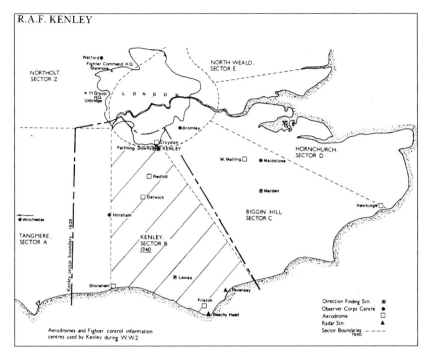

Plan showing Kenley Sector B. (P. Flint)

In June 1937 a new squadron was formed. 615 'County of Surrey' Army Co-operation Squadron of the Auxiliary Air Force was temporarily equipped with Hawker Hectors and Avro Tutor trainers and had Mr Winston Churchill as its honorary Air Commodore. By the end of the Battle of Britain it was to become known as 'Churchill's Own'.

Modernisation of the airfields was also in progress and to expand Kenley the old Handley Page and Vickers sheds were demolished and Hayes Lane, which divided the airfield, was rerouted.

March 1938 saw the new Hawker Hurricane monoplane fighters at Kenley, replacing the Gladiators of 3 Squadron, but almost immediately disaster struck. The high powered Hurricane with its coarse pitch propeller demanded a much longer take-off run and barely cleared the trees at the end of the Kenley runway. Two fatal crashes brought home the realisation that the airfield was too small to operate the Hurricanes, and its future lay in the balance. The Hurricanes were withdrawn to Biggin Hill and the Gladiators returned to 3 Squadron in July.

On 25th September 1938, with the worsening of the international situation, all leave at Kenley was stopped and all personnel on leave recalled. On the 26th the operations room was manned and the main Observer Corps posts at Horsham and Bromley were connected by telephone. 3 and 17 Squadrons were available and there was a scramble to paint the gleaming aircraft with the dull green and brown camouflage. Ammunition had to be belted and 615 Squadron moved out to Old Sarum. Then the Munich Crisis was averted and the Prime Minister returned to Britain proclaiming 'peace in our time'. The Kenley log on 1st October reported the political situation easing and things soon returned almost to normal. On the 4th, 615 Squadron returned and were converted to a fighter squadron, equipped with Gladiators.

In the uneasy peace that followed, the RAFVR were required to report to the Kenley operations room for training on three evenings per week, and for the civilian population the threat of war was always in mind. The presence of Air Raid Precaution Centres, issue of gas masks, and digging of air raid shelters heightened their apprehension and in this respect the Empire Air Day on 20th May 1939 held a particular significance as 14,000 of the public flocked to Kenley to see the latest the RAF had to offer.

By this time the future of Kenley had been decided. Two concrete runways were to be laid, increased in length to 800 yards to accommodate Hurricanes and Spitfires. This was to be made possible by the demolition of three of the existing seven hangars and in consequence 3 Squadron moved to Biggin Hill in May and 17 Squadron to North Weald, leaving only 615 Squadron in residence with their Gladiators. During August the aerodrome was out of use due to work on the runways and does not appear to have taken part in the greatest Annual Air Exercises ever held, from 8th to 11th August, testing the combined defences against air attack in a final rehearsal for the conflict to come.

On 24th August, with the political situation worsening, the Air Ministry ordered a state of readiness and the civil airports of Croydon and Gatwick were taken over as war stations. They became satellites of Kenley and on 1st September the general mobilisation of the RAF was ordered. The next few days at Kenley were hectic. Men and women reservists reported for duty, many without full kit, and all had to be found accommodation. The WAAF were billeted in the married quarters and Hillhurst, a large mansion house nearby, whilst the local church and tents were used by many airmen as temporary accommodation. The operations room was manned by RAF and RAFVR personnel along with liaison officers from the Army Commands, Observer Corps and RDF stations.

By 3rd September 1939 when war was declared all was ready yet Kenley, the Sector controlling station was non-operational except for the control room. 615 Squadron moved out to Croydon, to be joined by 3 and 17 Squadrons, now equipped with Hurricanes. This left the airfield without aircraft. It was fortunate that in the coming months of the 'Phoney War' construction work could continue without hindrance although it was hampered by the severe winter of 1940. At the end of January with construction work still not complete, 3 Squadron moved back from Croydon, to be joined at the end of March by B flight of 604 Squadron from Northolt. At last flying operations commenced, with Dover patrols and Channel escorts. By April Spitfires could use the airfield with caution and Kenley was fully operational, just in time!

On 10th May 1940 Germany attacked the Low Countries with a devastating blitzkrieg on the airfields of Holland, Belgium and France. This was followed by the Panzer divisions sweeping around the French Maginot Line, advancing with lightning speed and stopped only by the English Channel. The RAF had four Hurricane squadrons (including 615) and two Gladiator squadrons in France fighting alongside the other Allied air forces against overwhelming odds. The ferocity of the enemy attack and speed of advance across the Low Countries and France meant that more and more allied airfields, aircraft and equipment were being lost.

On the 10th, B flight of 604 Squadron from Kenley attacked forward German bases near The Hague, destroying four Junkers 52 troop carriers on the ground. On the same day 3 Squadron, along with a small fleet of Imperial Airways machines carrying vital spares, left Kenley for France as part of a force of 32 Hurricanes raised from different units, answering the cry for more aircraft replacements for the battered fighter squadrons. Kenley was now operating composite squadrons flying to France by day and returning at night.

On 18th May, 111 and 253 Squadrons were on the Cambrai/Le Cateau patrol when a large formation of enemy aircraft were encountered and in the ensuing fight five were destroyed. With fuel running low two aircraft flew directly back to Kenley whilst the remaining eight landed at Vitry for refuelling. Whilst they were preparing to take off the airfield was suddenly attacked and five Hurricanes were destroyed on the ground, the remaining three just making it back to Kenley. Two days later the situation was so bad that

3 Squadron operating from Merville had no alternative but to return to Kenley as their airfield became untenable, with the remnants of 2 and 615 Squadrons following behind.

At Kenley the remnants of the returning squadrons were formed into patrols, with flights from other squadrons flying in as reinforcements, and composites from 2, 17, 111, 229, 253 and 604 Squadrons flew over the towns of Calais and Dunkirk where the retreating Allied armies were massing. From 26th May, over Dunkirk, pilots reported seeing thousands of troops from the British Expeditionary Force and Allied armies swarming on the beaches below. Some were scrambling aboard ships of all shapes and sizes, under constant attack from dive-bombing and machine-gunning enemy aircraft.

The patrols of aircraft, in as many as 320 sorties a day, fought furious battles against the attacking Luftwaffe over the beachheads and further back into France, often unseen, in a valiant attempt to stop the enemy reaching the coast. The action lasted until 4th June when Operation Dynamo, the greatest evacuation of all time, was complete and 338,000 British and Allied troops had been landed in Britain – but at a cost. Beside the army and naval losses, since the German advance in May the RAF had lost 320 pilots killed or missing and over 950 aircraft, half its front line strength.

The fighting in France continued for a time and there were still British troops fighting back towards the Channel ports of Cherbourg and St Nazaire for evacuation back to Britain, with five Hurricane squadrons acting as cover. There were desperate pleas to send more fighter squadrons to France but in view of the extremely serious situation it was decided they could not be spared. On 17th June, France requested an armistice and by the 18th all organised fighting had stopped and the remains of the five squadrons rapidly made for home.

The situation was grim. Britain stood alone with the Luftwaffe now able to operate from bases in France, which meant that nowhere in Britain was out of range of the German bombers.

The defences at Kenley had been strengthened. There were now blastproof pens for the parking of aircraft at dispersal, air raid shelters for personnel, and sandbags and barbed wire everywhere. There were seven machine gun posts, four modern 40 mm Bofors guns for defence against low flying aircraft and two elderly three-inch AA guns. On the northern side was a new untried AA secret weapon, the parachute and cable system in which salvoes of rockets were fired in front of an enemy aircraft, trailing steel cables 480 feet long. When the parachutes opened the suspended cables would wrap around any attacking aircraft.

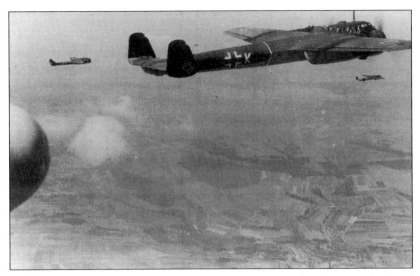

Dornier 17s 'Flying Pencil' of KG76 whose aircraft were used in the normal role and by the 9th Staffel who used them at low level as in the attack on Kenley. (MAP)

With the threat of invasion the main anxiety was of attack by parachute troops and extra Scots Guards were drafted in from Caterham Barracks with Bren and Lewis guns to bolster up the men of the Queen's Royal Regiment already on site. Many personnel were also issued with side arms. It was now a waiting game.

On 21st June a great boost for morale was the visit by HM King George VI accompanied by the AOC Fighter Command, Air Marshal Hugh Dowding. The King presented Squadron Leader J. Kayll, commanding officer of 615 Squadron, with the DSO and DFC, and the DFC to fellow pilot Flight Lieutenant Sanders.

Since the return of 615 Squadron from Belgium (the ground crew returned via Dunkirk) they had reformed and were joined by 64 Squadron's Spitfires, both flying shipping patrols from Hawkinge or Tangmere. They would fly down at first light and return at night. On the other side of the Channel the Luftwaffe were settling into their new bases in France, flying probing operations testing the British defences and attacking Channel shipping.

On 10th July 1940, a wet and cloudy morning, the Luftwaffe reconnaissance aircraft were about early. Around 10 am, in improving weather, a Dornier 17 of KG2 spotted a convoy below heading for the Dover Straits and immediately radioed its position back to base. The

Junkers 87 Stuka dive bomber. (MAP)

Dornier and its escort of Me 109s of 1/JG51 from Wissant were picked up on Dover radar and 74 Squadron's Spitfires from Manston were sent to intercept. The Dornier was shot down but the air battles continued throughout the day as the convoy forged its way through the Channel to Dover. Waves of Dorniers escorted by Me 109s and Me 110s of ZG26 from Wissant were beaten off by a total of five squadrons of Spitfires and Hurricanes sent to intercept them. The convoy reached Dover unscathed, the air battles broke up and the massive Luftwaffe force recrossed the Channel.

Goering had three Air Fleets mounted against Britain. Luftflotte 5 was in Norway, a small unit, and confronting us across the Channel were Luftflotte 2 in northern France under Generalfeldmarschall A. Kesselring, and Luftflotte 3 in western France, under Generalfeld-marschall H. Sperrle. Collectively, the Fleets could muster around 1,600 bombers and 1,100 fighters against Fighter Command's 700 Spitfires and Hurricanes. Daunting odds, but the outcome hinged really on how well Fighter Command dealt with the Me 109s and the twin engine Me 110s. The daily attacks on convoys and the Channel ports of Portland, Portsmouth and Dover by waves of Junkers 87 Stukas, Junkers 88s and Dornier 17s, protected by Messerschmitt 109 and 110 fighters, continued through July with the Kenley squadrons 64 and 615 alongside others beating off the attacks.

July 14th, a cloudy day, saw 615's first major encounter. Scrambled to patrol Hawkinge they were soon vectored to engage a large force of Ju 87s protected by Me 109s of Jagdgeschwader 3 from Wissant, who were dive-bombing a convoy off Portland. Pilot Officer Hugo fired at one Ju 87 but was going too fast and almost rammed it. He broke away but noted the rear gunner was not firing, and engaged another already attacked by Pilot Officer Collard. Transferring his attack back to the original Ju 87, Hugo dived steeply, firing short bursts and scoring hits all over the aircraft. Closing in to about 15 yards and buffeted by the slipstream, a final burst sent the flaming enemy aircraft into the sea where it sank. Collard also destroyed a Ju 87 but Pilot Officer Mudie was shot down in flames. He baled out and was rescued from the sea but sadly died next morning. Bad weather intervened but did not stop Hugo damaging a reconnaissance Do 17 which force-landed back in France.

On 20th July a convoy en route from Southend was attacked by Ju 87s of Stukageschwader G1 from Ghent protected by Me 109s of Jagdgeschwader 27 from Cherbourg. 615 scrambled from Hawkinge in good time and was joined by 32 Squadron. The latter destroyed two Ju

87s whilst Flight Lieutenant Gaunce, Pilot Officer Hugo and Flying Officer Eyre of 615 Squadron, attacking from a favourable position, each bagged an Me 109. By the end of the day the convoy got through for the loss of two ships. The Luftwaffe lost 13 aircraft whilst the RAF lost six.

By 1st August Hitler had realised that if German air supremacy was to be gained by Adler Tag, 13th August, then a change of tactics was imperative. In a directive he ordered the Luftwaffe to overpower the RAF with all the forces at its command in the shortest possible time. The attacks were now to be directed at airfields, communications, supply systems and aircraft production units.

On the 8th the escalation began with a massive attack on a convoy, code name Peewit, sustained during the night by E-boats and all day by waves of Ju 87s. The 11th saw the heaviest fighting of all over Weymouth and Portland with the enemy losing 38 aircraft. By the 12th it was realised in Germany that the only way to defeat the RAF was to destroy its greatest asset, the radar stations, and the attacks turned inland.

For these attacks the specialist unit, Erprobungsgruppe 210, consisting of Me 109 and Me 110 fighter bombers led by Hauptman Walter Rubensdörffer, set out and with unerring accuracy bombed the radar stations at Dunkirk, Pevensey, Rye and Dover. Buildings were destroyed, telephone lines ripped out and many personnel were killed but miraculously the open lattice-work towers survived the blast. Except for the Poling station, the 'eyes' of the RAF were out until back-ups could be brought into operation.

The weather on the 13th, Adler Tag, was not as predicted but a day of solid banks of cloud. Due to a technical problem the signals cancelling the German onslaught did not reach all the units who were already airborne heading for the airfields of Eastchurch, Middle Wallop, Rochester and Detling, and it was an inglorious day for the Luftwaffe. The 15th saw attacks mounted from bases in both Norway and France. From Luftflottes 5, 2 and 3 came the largest number of raids yet against the airfields and radar stations. West Malling was struck by Dorniers and Croydon was the target of a ferocious diving attack by Me 110s of Erpro 210. The enemy losses were heavy and the day became known as 'Black Thursday' by the Luftwaffe. Surprisingly 17th August, a brilliant day, was strangely quiet, with an air of unease.

Sunday, 18th August dawned a hot summer's day but a low haze over southern England delayed the take-off of nine Dornier 17s of the 9th Staffel of KG 76, from their airfield at Cormeilles, northern France until after midday when the visibility was expected to improve. The Staffel was a specialist low flying unit which had been very successful in France and today was part of a three-pronged attack, the objective to destroy Kenley.

The attack would be spearheaded by twelve Junkers 88s, followed by 27 Dornier 17s, all from KG 76. Bombing from high level, they planned to knock out the defences at Kenley and create havoc to allow a clear run for the low level attack to follow from the 9th Staffel, picking out any remaining targets to complete the destruction.

Just after 1 pm the high flying raiders had reached Ashford along with 60 Heinkel 111s bound for Biggin Hill and escorted by Messerschmitt 109s and 110s. The nine Dorniers of the 9th Staffel led by Hauptman Joachim Roth had war photographers and reporters on board and were taking another route, skimming the Channel at 50 feet, under the radar screen. Crossing the English coast at Cuckmere, Roth picked up the railway to the Burgess Hill junction and then the main Brighton line north to London. Jinking at 50 feet above the rooftops, hopeful to avoid detection, their plan was foiled by the ever vigilant Observer Corps who monitored their route.

In the control room at Kenley the two converging raids had been noted, the high level to the east, and the low level to the south. Their intentions were clear. The station defences were mounted, and the controller, Anthony Norman, scrambled 64 and 615 Squadrons to patrol overhead at 20,000 and 25,000 feet to intercept the high flying raid. At Croydon the controller, sensing the situation, scrambled 111 Squadron's Hurricanes to patrol at 3,000 feet.

At about 1.20 pm the nine Dorniers passed over Bletchingly, spot on time, with only two minutes to go. Their leader Roth looked towards Kenley for tell tale signs of smoke rising from the high level attacks but there was none. Realising something was wrong, he had no alternative but to continue the attack alone.

The Staffel split into three flights and, with Roth leading, cleared the last of the high ground and swooped at 50 feet over the Kenley hangars. They were met by an unexpected barrage of fire from the four Bofors guns, AA guns and machine guns from the various posts around. Their 20 110 lb low-level bombs crashed into hangars, sick quarters and other buildings whilst some bounced like rubber balls along the runways. The hangars collapsed like matchwood sending sheets of flame and smoke into the air.

The Dorniers sped on, returning fire from their machine guns and cannon, the airfield criss-crossed with lines of tracer. A Dornier was hit

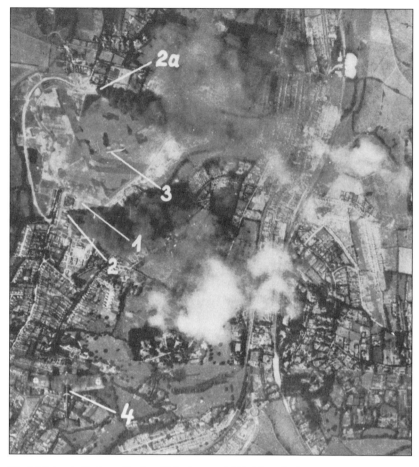

The high level attack on Kenley, 18th August 1940. Note the Dornier 17 below (4). (F. Cheesman)

and on fire but their trouble was only beginning. Diving down from above, the Hurricanes of 111 Squadron were curving in behind for the attack.

Suddenly, rising from the ground on the north side of the aerodrome, in front of the fleeing Dorniers were terrifying balls of red fire from the PAC rockets, below which were suspended long steel cables. Roth's pilot, Oberleutnant Lamberty, climbed to avoid the cables but his aircraft was immediately hit in the left wing, ripping out the petrol tank and causing the aircraft to catch fire. The first Dornier hit tangled with

114

a cable and dropped out of control onto a bungalow called Sunnycroft outside the aerodrome. Two other aircraft were hit, one seriously wounding the pilot, which left the inexperienced navigator wrestling with the controls to prevent it crashing. The remaining Dorniers sped for home.

The lead Hurricane sped low over the mayhem below in chase but before he could engage, Flight Lieutenant Stanley Connors' aircraft was hit by machine gun fire. Turning away it crashed, killing the pilot. The following Hurricanes climbed above the battle to swoop down when clear.

Meanwhile, the high flying raid was late approaching Kenley and the escort was being attacked by 615 and 32 Squadrons from Biggin Hill. 64 Squadron was awaiting the main bomber stream but, answering the call from the controller of 'Bandits overhead', Squadron Leader Don MacDonell took 64 down in a long spiral and soon became engaged in the melee of aircraft below.

MacDonell latched on to an Me 110 and hit it with a burst from 250 yards. With both engines on fire it reared up, stalled and spun down through 6,000 feet. Seemingly finished, it straightened out and with both engines smoking made for home.

The Ju 88s arriving last of all decided there was too much smoke over the target to accurately dive bomb, and diverted their attack onto West Malling and Croydon. Far below, 111 Squadron was chasing the low flying Dorniers (see Croydon).

Pilot Officer 'Dutch' Hugo of A flight, 615 Squadron was circling at 25,000 feet above his own aerodrome, waiting to take on the fighter escort. Suddenly he spotted Me 109s coming out of the sun fast. A Hurricane alongside belonging to Sergeant Walley went down in flames and Hugo turned to engage and was hit. Wounded, with the cockpit swilling in petrol and the aircraft spinning, he decided it was time to leave. A sudden bang on the head from another attack knocked him out. Coming round with the aircraft still spinning, he tried to get out but the harness was caught up and he fell back. Continuing his descent, he successfully put the battered Hurricane down in a field near Orpington and was rushed to hospital.

Flight Lieutenant Elmer Gaunce, a member of A flight, was hit and with his Hurricane on fire, baled out and landed safely. Another 615 pilot, Pilot Officer D. Looker, was also hit by the surprise attack of the Me 109s. Breaking away he made for an emergency landing at Croydon only to be hailed by a barrage from the home gunners. He landed, tipping the aircraft up on its nose. Sergeant Walley's Hurricane, the

An airman reflects on the wreckage of a hangar after the attack on 18th August 1940. (Imperial War Museum)

first of A flight to be hit, crashed out of control on Morden Park golf course with the unfortunate pilot still inside.

615 Squadron had suffered terribly but their fight with the top cover Me 109s had allowed 64 and 32 Squadrons to engage the bombers below, breaking up their attack on Kenley aerodrome. On the credit side Flight Lieutenant Sanders claimed a He 111 and a Ju 88 and another Ju 88 in partnership with another Hurricane, and Squadron Leader Joe Kayll an Me 109, with other aircraft damaged by 615 Squadron pilots.

The lunchtime raiders were chased hard across Kent to the Channel and losses were high on both sides. Fighter Command lost 25 fighters (eight on the ground) and 18 damaged whilst the raiders lost 21 aircraft and 15 damaged.

The first raid at Kenley took two minutes and the second ten to fifteen minutes and approximately 100 HE bombs were dropped, 24 of which were delayed action. Three hangars were destroyed, the sick quarters and a nearby shelter suffered direct hits and most other buildings were damaged but miraculously the operations room was left standing with one telephone line to the outside still working. Fire engines and motor vehicles were destroyed and ten aeroplanes were

The Kenley operations centre, a standard type building protected only by an earth bank. Although it escaped serious damage during the air attack, it was thought to be too vulnerable and moved to 'Camp B', a shop in Caterham. (P. Flint)

destroyed on the ground, six of which were 615 Hurricanes, with several others damaged.

Rescuers worked feverishly to free trapped victims in the sick quarters and shelters. 615's Medical Officer, Flight Lieutenant Crombie, was killed when the sick quarters were hit. Fire and rescue services soon arrived and an emergency medical centre was set up in the one remaining hangar. Royal Engineers began to deal with the unexploded bombs and stock piles of rubble were used to fill in bomb craters on runways and roads. The returning Kenley squadrons were diverted to Croydon and Redhill whilst a runway was made serviceable.

Kenley had been devastated. The Luftwaffe had achieved their objective but at a high price with the 9th Staffel losing four aircraft, two seriously damaged and the remaining three lightly damaged.

Immediately after the raid RAF personnel and civilian teams worked through the day and night and by the next day the airfield was back in business putting up patrols. 64 Squadron left for a well earned rest and were replaced by 616 Squadron from Leconfield, who arrived to a scene greatly different from the one they had left in Yorkshire. A few days of bad weather gave a welcome respite and helped to consolidate forces for the heavy fighting to come at the end of the month. Always a morale booster, the Prime Minister, Mr Winston Churchill paid a visit to see his squadron under active service conditions.

When fighting resumed losses were high on both sides. On one day, the 26th, the Kenley squadrons took a fearful mauling when 616 lost seven Spitfires and 615, four Hurricanes. Dowding was extremely worried about the loss of pilots, faster than replacements could be trained, and called heavily on pilots from Army Co-operation, Bomber and Coastal Commands and the Fleet Air Arm.

At the end of the month 615 left their battered but beloved home for

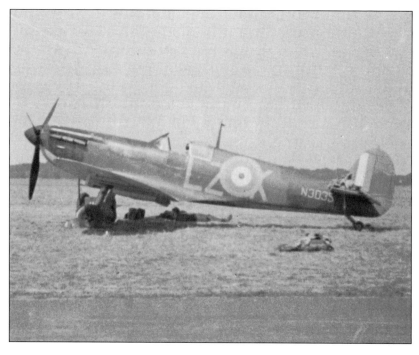

Flight Lieutenant H. R. Allen's Spitfire, of 66 Squadron, September 1940 at the ready, with "trolley-acc" plugged in and pilot waiting. (Wing Commander Allen, DFC)

118

Prestwick after a very long period of active service. The movement of the operations room from its vulnerable position on the airfield was given top priority and it was resited at Camp B, a butcher's shop in Caterham, where it remained effectively until December. At the same time, 253 Squadron arrived equipped with Hurricanes.

On 1st September the Luftwaffe mounted another attack on Kenley with eight bombers and 50 fighters at high level. Little damage was done to the airfield but there was substantial damage to surrounding areas.

Two days later a badly depleted 616 Squadron left Kenley and 66 Squadron arrived from Coltishall with their Spitfires. They were immediately in the thick of it, losing ten Spitfires in the first two days. The loss was soon redressed on 4th September by 253 and 66 Squadrons, 253 destroying six Me 110s and 66 a Me 109. They also damaged others without loss to themselves.

The emergency operations room at Camp B in Caterham was now operational, relaying instructions to ground and gun crews by tannoy and by telephone to the hut alongside the waiting aircraft at dispersal. The pilots at readiness sitting in the summer sun or in the hut awaited the order over the telephone to 'scramble' accompanied by the loud ringing of a handbell by the ground controller.

Life was hard at Kenley for everyone and letters home by a young engine fitter serving with 66 Squadron were typical: '. . . there is hardly anything left standing . . . what a cheerful place this is. We get nothing but air raid warnings . . . all round the station are speakers giving instructions to pilots and ground guns. We have to work out in the open to do the maintenance work, there are no hangars . . . but the weather is lovely . . .'.

On 7th September the raids switched to London. The Docks, the East End and Woolwich Arsenal were the main targets for a terrible attack causing great fires. At about 4 pm a force of some 400 Dorniers and Heinkels, in waves accompanied by 600 fighters, crossed the coast bound for the capital. Watching this great aerial armada from the clifftops of Cap Gris Nez was Hermann Goering, who was now personally directing the operation.

Around 4.20 pm, 11 Group scrambled 22 squadrons. At Kenley, 253 were airborne at 4.25 and 66 at 4.45, but despite furious fighting the bomber force got through to discharge its evil load, the pillars of smoke blotting out the sun.

In the afternoon that young fitter who wrote home had seen off Pilot Officer C. Bodie in Spitfire LZ/F of 66 Squadron. Over Folkestone

Bodie was suddenly surrounded by Me 109s, his aircraft was hit and he was forced down. Gliding down into the haze with wheels and flaps lowered, he made an approach into a small field but, crossing the hedge, a large wood loomed up only 200 yards away. Sensing danger he whipped the wheels up and the aircraft pancaked only 100 yards from the trees.

There were other smaller diversionary raids but the main bomber force returned to the Continent at nightfall, discharging what was left of their deadly cargo into the fires raging below. They flew almost with impunity, the coastal radar not being accurate enough to direct night fighters and the Observer Corps, in the darkness, just listening to the throb of the aircraft engines. The only defence was the AA barrage, impressive but not very effective.

The switch to night raiding directed at the civil population was the pattern of things to come and would last for the next eight months or so. The Blitz against London and other cities had begun. Terrible as it was, it took the pressure off the airfields, enabling them to re-establish, a tactical mistake the Germans would regret.

The frequency and scale of daylight raids diminished in the next

Pilots and Hurricane of 501 Squadron, the commanding officer, Squadron Leader Hogan seventh from left, Sept/Oct 1940. (Surrey Local Studies Library)

week allowing Dowding a breathing space to reorganise 11 Group. On 10th September a battle-worn 66 Squadron moved to Gravesend and 501 replaced them at Kenley, which was now operating all Hurricanes. The decisive day was yet to come and on 15th September 1940 the Battle of Britain reached a climax.

The dawn of a beautiful autumn day with clear blue skies brought the Luftwaffe reconnaissance planes about early. Dowding, sensing a build up of activity, had reinforced 11 Group with additional squadrons from 10 and 12 Groups and recalled squadrons away resting. About 11 am radar reported increased activity in the Pas de Calais and by noon, all 23 squadrons had been scrambled ready to intercept the coming raid. The Kenley squadrons 253 and 501 were airborne at 11.20, and 605 joined them from Croydon. By chance the Prime Minister, Mr Winston Churchill was visiting 11 Group HQ and as the raid was mounted turned to AVM Keith Park, AOC 11 Group and asked, 'What reserves have we?' Park replied, 'There are none!'

The first raid of 40-plus bombers, mainly from III/KG76 at Beauvais and Cormeilles with an escort of JG3 Me 109s, crossed the coast at about 11.30 am for 'one last great effort'. They were met with a head-on attack by Hurricanes of 253 and 501 Squadrons. This kind of attack had been pioneered by Squadron Leader 'Gerry' Edge, commanding officer of Kenley's 253 and on this occasion ten Hurricanes knocked out 17 Dorniers from a bunch of 28. They were not all destroyed but the formation was broken up and other squadrons joined in, scattering the raiders who dropped their bombs indiscriminately before fleeing for home.

In the afternoon a bigger raid developed, when 150 to 200 Dorniers and Heinkels of KG53, KG2 and KG56, escorted by twice as many Me 109s and Me 110s, crossed the coast in three waves at around 2 pm bound for London. Approaching the capital, they were set upon by over 170 Spitfires and Hurricanes intent on destroying the invaders who had wreaked such cruelty on the Londoners. Guarded by the fighter escort of Adolf Galland's Me 109s, the bombers were difficult to engage until the enemy fighters ran low on fuel and turned for home, leaving the bombers prey to the Spitfires and Hurricanes. The final hammer blow was the arrival of Douglas Bader's Duxford Wing of five squadrons. The enemy formations broke up, jettisoning their bombs over a wide area and sped home.

From the ground Londoners gazed up at the white contrails against the blue sky, made by the aircraft wheeling and diving at such a height they were almost invisible to the eye. The rise and fall of aero engines and the sound of machine gun fire could be heard, as could the whine and crash of bombs and the bits falling from spent bullets and shrapnel making a loud crack as they hit the roofs of houses.

In the evening the wireless reported that 185 enemy aircraft were destroyed (later revised to 56) but it was not the number of aircraft lost by itself that was important but the effect on the morale of the Luftwaffe. They had been told the RAF could be 'broken in four days', but they now appeared stronger than ever. The Germans had thrown in all they had, and for 11 Group it was indeed make or break but the defences were held by the gallant 'few'. The Kenley squadrons' part was twelve aircraft destroyed, with seven damaged for the loss of three pilots and aircraft. On 17th September Hitler postponed the invasion indefinitely and thus perished Operation Sealion. In retrospect, 15th September is now regarded as the day the battle was won and is honoured as Battle of Britain Day.

The day raids now continued on a reduced and more diverse scale. Fighter aircraft production units were singled out as prime targets. The Dorniers and Heinkels were replaced by fighter bombers, Me 109s and Me 110s carrying 500 lb bombs and Ju 88s used as dive bombers. Fast, high flying and effective, once they had released their bombs the Me 109s and Me 110s became highly effective fighters, hoping to draw the RAF into the air. Often used singly they would slip in under low cloud, find their target and speed away.

As the autumn weather closed in the daylight raids tailed off but the night raids continued with savage attacks on London and other cities. Kenley, lying under the route of the night raiders, often received attention from the aircraft passing overhead. On 29th September incendiary bombs were dropped; on 17th October nine aircraft were damaged by HE bombs; and on 12th November a lone raider bombed the last remaining hangar, destroying a searchlight post on the corner of the building, damaging sleeping quarters and killing two soldiers and wounding four other personnel.

In November the emergency operations building in Caterham, Camp B, was closed and a new one was opened in Old Coulsdon, known as Camp C. A large house, The Grange, had been taken over and in the summer the interior was converted into a spacious control room. With a high ceiling, it was fitted out in the usual style with a raised gallery from which the controllers could look down onto a large table holding a map of southern England and France. It was on this that the WAAF plotters continuously marked the position of aircraft. However, moving back closer to the airfield brought its risks for on 1st December in the morning two high flying aircraft dropped three bombs close to the building.

As the night raids persisted the use of night fighters was given top priority, and the need arose to develop the use of Airborne Interception Radar. Redhill had been selected in preference to Croydon to operate 600 and later 219 Squadrons' Blenheim IVs and Beaufighter Is equipped with early AI radar. Redhill, however, was prone to become muddy in wet weather and when this happened Kenley would accept a flight on standby, making use of the hard runways.

253 and 501 Squadrons stayed until December when 615 returned to its home base at Kenley and, after a well earned Christmas dinner and break, 1 Squadron flew in and Kenley prepared for offensive operations. In November Air Marshal Sir William Sholto Douglas had taken over as AOC Fighter Command and was advocating a policy of 'Leaning forward into France', taking the fight to the enemy.

On 9th January 1941 the Kenley Wing of nine Hurricanes of 1 Squadron and twelve Hurricanes of 615 led by Wing Commander John Peel flew the first offensive patrol along the French coast from Cap Gris Nez to Calais. No enemy aircraft were seen but it was good to be back over France!

The second sortie on 2nd February was a Circus operation, when 1 Squadron along with 303, 601 and three Spitfire squadrons from Biggin Hill, escorted six Blenheims to bomb the port of Boulogne. The prime object of the Circus, a small force of bombers escorted by a large number of fighters, was to provoke a response from enemy fighters, the aim being to destroy as many as possible. Eight Me 109s attacked but there were no losses.

Three days later 1, 302 and 615 Squadrons escorted twelve Blenheims on a Circus to bomb St Omer aerodrome, where 1 encountered their first loss when Pilot Officer Lewis's Hurricane was hit and with the engine on fire he parachuted into the Channel. Despite efforts by Squadron Leader Brown a rescue boat could not be raised.

The conditions for air fighting had now changed. During the Battle of Britain British pilots had operated over home territory and a forced or parachute landing was on friendly soil but now there was the added danger of landing on occupied territory or at best in the Channel.

If the weather was bad with low cloud the more dangerous Rhubarb operations were flown. On 8th February six Hurricanes of 1 Squadron flew under the cloud base at low level and attacked the airfield at Invercampf and invasion barges at Dunkirk.

British fighters were now operating over France in stronger numbers

Hurricane I of 615 Squadron, belonging to the commanding officer, Wing Commander R. A. Holmwood – it has the commanding officer's pennant on the rear of the cockpit. It was shot down on 26th February 1941 and Holmwood was killed. (Imperial War Museum)

but they still had to deal with nuisance raids by the Luftwaffe, mainly by high flying Me 109s over the south of England. On 26th February 1941 tragedy struck for 615 Squadron. In the afternoon seven Hurricanes of B flight, in vics of three with a weaver at the back, were scrambled to patrol the Dover/Folkestone area and vectored to intercept Me 109s at 30,000 feet. Whilst climbing they were suddenly attacked from behind by Me 109s and two Hurricanes were seen to fall, one on fire. Pilot Officer Foxley-Norris baled out of one and landed safely but Wing Commander R. A. Holmwood, RAAF, the commanding officer of 615, whilst baling out of his burning aircraft was tragically killed when his parachute caught fire. Another Hurricane force-landed, but the pilot, although wounded, survived. It was a sad day for 615.

In the coming weeks the Kenley Wing were engaged on shipping patrols and Roadstead operations (anti shipping strikes), until 21st April when there was a change of squadrons: 1 went to Croydon, whilst 615 left their home base for the last time. 258 replaced them from Valley, with 302 (Polish) Squadron joining as an additional squadron. 1 then returned to Redhill as a night fighter squadron. The Kenley Wing was now firmly established, which would set the pattern for some time. Three squadrons, two based at Kenley and one at Redhill, rotated with

The flight commanders of 452 Squadron, autumn 1941 – Keith 'Bluey' Truscott, DFC and Bar; 'Paddy' Finucane, DFC and Bar; and Ray Thorold Smith, DFC. (Surrey County Libraries)

each one having a spell of duty at Redhill.

The first operation for the new Wing was a Circus on the night of 10th May to Bethune, with 258 flying close escort, 302 medium cover and 1 Squadron as high cover. The close cover role was the most hated, the escort staying tight to the bombers and becoming prey to any enemy aircraft breaking through the free-ranging top cover and then through the medium cover. A large number of enemy aircraft were encountered and two Me 109s were destroyed with four damaged by 1 Squadron and one probable by 302.

The offensive operations were stepped up and in June the Hurricane squadrons were replaced by the Spitfire IIas of 452 (RAAF), 485 (RNZAF), and 602 'City of Glasgow' Squadrons.

The Wing was heavily engaged, sometimes flying two operations a day. In July, 33 Circus operations were flown against short range targets in northern France but August saw the first encounters with the new Focke-Wulf 190 which was far superior to the ageing Spitfire IIa. Sadly, casualties began to rise. There was, however, some improvement when the Spitfire IIas were replaced with the more powerful

Spitfire Vb equipped with two 20 mm Hispano cannon and four .303 Browning machine guns, but still it was not a match for the superb Fw 190.

During August 1941 Johnny Kent took over as Wing Commander Flying, and Flight Lieutenant 'Paddy' Finucane came to Kenley as Flight Commander of 452 Squadron, later taking over command of 602 from Squadron Leader Al Deere. Paddy Finucane rapidly became famous for his skill as a top scoring fighter pilot and his exploits were followed by the general public in newspapers and on the wireless. A great fillip to the morale of the nation. Promoted to Wing Commander, he took over the Hornchurch Wing but soon after was tragically lost in the Channel. Not in a fight but by a piece of stray shrapnel from an AA battery striking his glycol tank. He was last seen and heard gliding his Spitfire down to crash in the sea but despite a long search by his circling comrades he could not be found.

At the beginning of 1942, Group Captain Victor Beamish took over the command of the Kenley Sector. A highly respected man, he enjoyed the affection of everyone around him. At the age of 39 he still flew operations with his pilots although leaving the control of the Wing to the Wing Commander Flying.

On 12th February Kenley Wing, comprising 452, 485 and 602 Squadrons, had the task of escorting Beaufort torpedo bombers on a Roadstead anti-shipping strike, but the weather was bad with low cloud and rain which made the rendezvous impossible. The Wing, now led by Wing Commander Boyd accompanied by Group Captain Beamish, decided to press on and when nearing the French coast two Me 109Fs were spotted and chased. On nearing the Berck/Le Touquet area, to their amazement they saw below in the gloom a large fleet of two battleships (the *Scharnhorst* and *Gneisenau*), a heavy cruiser (*Prinz Eugen*), three destroyers, twelve E-boats and troop transports, escorted by twelve Me 109s of JG2 and JG26. Signalling the attack, the Wing let fly with cannon and machine gun fire, raking the enemy ships from stem to stern. Beamish and Boyd sank two E-boats then, obeying radio silence, returned to the nearest aerodrome to report the find.

The report triggered a contingency operation codenamed Fuller. The German fleet had left the French port of Brest overnight heading for Norway, and hoped to make a dash through the Channel in daylight. The first attack at 12.25 pm mounted by the Fleet Air Arm from Manston was by six Fairey Swordfish torpedo bombers of 825 Squadron led by Lieutenant Commander Eugene Esmonde. No hits were recorded and all six aircraft were lost. For this heroic attack

Pilots of 401 Squadron, the first Canadians to be stationed at Kenley in April 1942. (Imperial War Museum)

Esmonde was awarded a posthumous VC.

The Kenley Wing were airborne again at 1.27 pm but once again failed to rendezvous with Beauforts carrying torpedoes and carried on alone. 452 and 602 Squadrons spotted the ships in appalling weather and came through heavy flak to strafe troop ships crowded with men whilst 602 attacked a destroyer but without success. Meanwhile, over Ostende 485 had encountered a heavy enemy fighter escort and a furious scrap ensued. One Fw 190 and three Me 109s were destroyed. All through the day attacks were made by a total of 675 aircraft but disastrously the fleet escaped in the low mist and rain; 44 aircraft were lost against the enemy's 17 fighters.

Operations now took the squadrons deeper into France and although enemy fighter presence was reduced due to the German involvement on the Russian Front, they became more hazardous. The enemy fighters could pick their opportunities, often positioning up-sun. On 28th March the Kenley Wing accompanied by Group Captain Beamish set out for France with 485 Squadron at 18,000 feet, 457 at 19,000 feet, and 602 at 20,000 feet. Making a landfall just south of Cap Gris Nez at 5.34 pm, they were attacked from above by 50 enemy aircraft. Beamish turned to intercept but was himself attacked by two Fw 190s. Flight

A Spitfire Mk IX, the counter to the Fw 190, used by the Kenley squadrons later in the war. (MAP)

Lieutenant Grant of 485 rendered prompt assistance, probably destroying one and certainly damaging another, but he lost sight of Beamish who was last seen heading out to sea, his aircraft trailing a little smoke.

During many ensuing combats that day the Kenley Wing destroyed eleven enemy aircraft, with four probable and five damaged. Their leader and three other pilots failed to return. 602 took off at 7 pm in an endeavour to find the missing pilots and at 7 am next day 602 and 485 searched for many hours but no trace of them was found.

Group Captain R. A. Atcherly took over command of the Sector and in July B. Kingcombe took over as Wing Commander Flying from E. P. Wells. Then, in August 1942, the American Air Force arrived with 4 and 308 Fighter Squadrons. They came to gain experience in escorting Fortresses on their daylight bombing raids. Lacking suitable fighters of their own, the Americans borrowed some Spitfire Vbs which were available now that the Kenley Squadrons were equipping with the new Spitfire Mark IXs. At last the Spitfire pilots could meet the Fw 190 on equal or better terms. The Mark IX with the Merlin engine uprated to 1,710 hp from the 1,440 hp of the Mark Vb could now attain 416 mph at 27,500 feet.

In the week leading up to 19th August rumours abounded that a special operation was afoot and this was confirmed when additional

A Spitfire Mk V of 111 Squadron with a Norwegian pilot, 24th August 1942. (Imperial War Museum)

squadrons arrived at Redhill and Kenley. All leave was stopped and security tightened. On 18th August Spitfires of 611 had swept the beaches from Dieppe to Le Havre attacking gun posts and fortifications as a prelude to Operation Jubilee. The next day heralded the Allies' return to France when a combined operation by 6,000 Canadian troops attempted to capture Dieppe and hold it until midday.

Immense air support cover was employed and the Kenley squadrons were operating all day. 111 Squadron took off at 4.16 am in the dark to patrol the landing area followed by 308 (USAAF), 350 (Belgian), 402 (Canadian) and 611 Squadrons. The landing operation went badly and many troops were lost, killed or taken prisoner. In addition to the fighter cover over the beaches and shipping, the Kenley squadrons escorted Fortresses to bomb the fighter airfield at Abbeville. During this raid the Americans gained some of their earliest experience, with First Lieutenant Hill probably destroying an Fw 190. All squadrons were engaged in heavy fighting, seven enemy aircraft were destroyed and twelve damaged for the loss of one pilot.

The year continued with Circus operations escorting Fortresses and

Wing Commander 'Johnnie' Johnson, commanding officer of the Canadian Wing, with colleagues. (Imperial War Museum)

the smaller Bostons on daylight bombing missions, and also saw the arrival of more Canadian squadrons, eventually forming an all Canadian Wing. In March 1943 this Wing was taken over by Wing Commander 'Johnnie' Johnson from Wing Commander K. Hodson.

The weather on Johnson's arrival was bad and it was three weeks into April before an improvement meant a sortie could be flown to see how the Wing performed. The first was a simple operation escorting a squadron of Typhoons at low level to bomb the airfield at Abbeville. The Wing was to climb to high level and attack any Me 109s and Fw 190s flushed out by the bombing.

As they crossed the coast to the south of Le Touquet they saw the Typhoons leaving below. On reaching 24,000 feet the controller called to report 20-plus bandits climbing and gave a vector. From then on he continued to give plots, working the Wing around to bring them out of the sun.

Suddenly the controller called: 'Greycap, bandits now seven miles ahead, 5,000 feet below. Gate! [max speed]'.

The Spitfires were put into a dive, the leader searching for the enemy, when a call from a radar station warned of another enemy force behind at five to eight miles, closing. The enemy came into sight below. The decision was made, the order given to attack, and the Spitfires continued their dive. The co-ordinated attack was now for individual pilots to pick their own targets. Johnson picked an Fw 190, missing with the first burst, but the second hit the wing root and the aircraft went down on fire.

Another warning from the controller: 'Greycap, strong force of bandits approaching, almost on top of you'. Given the order to withdraw the Spitfires, nose down, sped for home. Twenty three landed, one aircraft was missing. The operation had been a success and the Wing behaved splendidly with six Fw 190s destroyed.

The successful operations of the Wing continued throughout the summer of 1943, escorting large formations of American Fortresses deeper into Germany, yet keeping at a respectful distance as the American gunners let fly at anything approaching! As their range became greater than that of the Spitfire, the long range American Thunderbolts and Mustang fighters were taking over.

Plans for the invasion of Europe were in hand and by August the 2nd Tactical Air Force headquarters had been formed and was absorbing squadrons from Fighter Command to form mobile airfields, whose purpose would be to follow the invasion fleet. The Kenley Canadian Wing of 403 and 421 (RCAF) Squadrons was formed into No 127 Airfield and moved out into the rural new Advanced Landing Ground at Lashenden near Headcorn in Kent. Gone were the comfortable messes at Kenley and life was now under canvas with food served from a mobile field kitchen. This was conditioning for the times which lay ahead.

Their stay would not be for long but in the meantime 66 and 165 Squadrons moved into Kenley as part of the Air Defence of Great Britain and continued to escort American bombers, mainly Marauders. The squadrons also operated from the Sector forward base of Friston, perched high on the cliffs overlooking the sea at the Seven Sisters in Sussex.

By October No 127 Airfield returned to Kenley, now commanded by Wing Commander Godefroy. They stayed until 18th April 1944 when 403, 416 and 421 (RCAF) Squadrons moved out to Tangmere with its servicing wing in preparation for the invasion of Europe on 6th June 1944.

It was not realised at the time that the days of operational flying at Kenley were over. Consequent to the departure, the strength of the airfield decreased along with its activity. Its reduction in status was only realised when the Sector was taken over by Biggin Hill.

On 15th June the V1 attacks began and Biggin Hill Station Flight used the airfield, but as the launching sites of the flying bombs moved, the flight paths overflew Kenley and flying ceased. The base now became a Disarmament School training personnel for a move into Europe when the war ended to take over captured war material.

In September 1945, with the war over, a small band of Air Ministry scientists moved in to supervise the storage and disposal of German aircraft equipment sent over by the Disarmament units. For a few months Kenley was part of 46 Group Transport Command, and then headquarters of No 6 Group, Reserve Command. In July 1946 615 Squadron, 'County of Surrey', was reformed not at Kenley but at Biggin Hill. The airfield's proximity to London was now an objection and its small size precluded its consideration for handling the new generation of jet fighters.

In 1949 Royal Auxiliary Air Force, Army Observer Post Squadron No 661 was formed and flew Tiger Moths and Austers until the Auxiliary squadrons were disbanded in 1957. The airfield closed in March 1974 but gliding for the Air Training Corps had always been a feature and still continues.

Flying over Kenley today, little has changed of its general appearance apart from the absence of buildings. The hard runways and perimeter track are still there but gliders now rest upon the grass where once the Hurricanes and Spitfires stood.

6
FAIROAKS

A small grass airfield two miles north of Woking and four miles west of Brooklands, Fairoaks was non-operational during the war but was instead a very busy pilot training centre vital to the war effort. It was also a repair centre for damaged Bristol aeroplanes.

Fairoaks was operated by General Aircraft Ltd under the control of Flying Training Command. With the RAF expansion scheme in the 1930s, on 2nd October 1937 No 18 Elementary & Reserve Flying Training School was started at Fairoaks to train RAFR, RAFO and RAFVR pilots under the direction of the Superintendent of Reserve at Hendon. The school was managed by Flight Lieutenant H. A. Schofield, RAFO, of Schneider Trophy fame.

The first intake of pupils were 24 volunteer reserve students, together with six DH 82a Tiger Moths. Tiger Moths continued to be used during the war at Fairoaks as the 'workhorse' for initial training. They were two-seater tandem biplanes, with a 130 hp Gipsy Major engine giving a maximum speed of 104 mph. Although they were fairly easy aircraft to fly, to fly them well and accomplish a good landing required a delicate touch.

The school soon became very busy and in its first year the students completed some 3,000 hours flying. The number of pupils increased to 70 and the training fleet added two more Tiger Moths, four Hawker Hinds, four Hawker Audaxes and four Hawker Hind LBs. As war loomed the number of flying instructors rose to ten, plus a sergeant Link trainer instructor.

On 1st September 1939, with war imminent, No 19 E&RFTS at Gatwick under Flight Lieutenant Bennet was transferred to Fairoaks complete with pupils and staff. When their course ended on 9th October, they were sent for advanced training at South Cerney and the instructors, now surplus to requirements, were gradually posted away to the Central Flying School. At the same time, after a great deal of

No 18 E&RFTS Tiger Moths and Hawker Hinds in the main hangar. (A. Milton)

uncertainty, the flying instructors at Fairoaks were mobilised. They still remained employees of the company, however, and the school became No 18 Elementary Flying Training School.

By 20th October the school had settled down to a wartime routine and No 1 War Course began with 29 pupils. However, it was soon realised that training was taking far too long and over the next few months the duration of the course was reduced to six weeks. There was no restriction on the hours flown but pupils were limited to one hour and ten minutes per day. By the time the course ended they would have gone solo and carried out some local flying and a cross-country exercise, or they would have failed. At the end of the course the aptitude of the pupil for further training was assessed and they were sent to either a single-engine training school for possible fighter training or to a twin-engine school for bomber or transport training. The length of the courses continued to shorten as the war progressed, and the number of pupils per course increased to over 50.

Pupils were sent on local flying exercises and expected to follow the rules. Woe betide anyone found guilty of low flying, but inevitably many became 'uncertain of their position' and force-landed in a field. The problem was compounded by the removal of all road signs and

134

names as a wartime defence measure and pupils often had to ask where they were and where the nearest telephone was before they could contact Fairoaks for help.

In May 1940 with the Battle of Britain already raging overhead and the fear of imminent invasion, instructions were issued to obstruct the aerodrome and all meadow land within a four mile radius of the airfield with scrap motor cars. This was to prevent enemy gliders and aircraft landing and was obviously impractical during the day, but every night after flying ceased it was 'all hands to the pumps' as 50 old cars, some with engines missing, were towed by tractors or manhandled into place. This carried on until the onset of wet weather when the grass surface became badly cut up, whereupon it was discontinued.

In the summer it was decided to equip all training aircraft with racks for 20-25 lb bombs in case of grave emergency. Five pilots carried out a practice scheme dive-bombing the centre of the airfield and afterwards two flights were formed for this purpose. Fortunately, they were never used.

On 4th September 1940, Brooklands aerodrome four miles to the east was the victim of a savage and unexpected air attack with very heavy casualties. Eyewitnesses at Fairoaks remember hearing the explosions

Fairoaks was a busy repair site for Bristol aircraft, amongst which was the Beaufighter. (MAP)

135

and seeing the German aircraft approaching Fairoaks on the way home. Suspecting a further raid, everyone made for cover whilst the airfield defences let fly with everything they had. There was a lot of noise and confusion but the airfield escaped. Afterwards Hurricanes manufactured at Brooklands were flown in to Fairoaks and dispersed in the wooded area around the airfield for comparative safety.

Battle-damaged Bristol aircraft were now arriving and were received in the new hangars built on the other side of the road past the airfield. They would arrive on Queen Mary road transporters in a sorry state and after offloading were stripped down for repair – Blenheims at first, then Beauforts and Beaufighters. Some, if not too badly damaged, flew in. The fuselages were repaired and then wheeled across the road to the other hangars where the wings and engines were reassembled after overhaul. Finally, they were taken up to the spray shop near the control tower for repainting. After repair the aircraft were test flown either by the chief test pilot of Faireys or by Wing Commander Arthur, the chief flying instructor of the flying school, and then parked up awaiting collection. Later the Fairchild Argus would arrive from White Waltham carrying the ferry pilots, many of them women, from the Air Transport Auxiliary who would fly them to service aerodromes. As far as can be ascertained only one accident occurred on this ferry service after repair, when a Beaufort taking off had an engine fire and, turning back to the airfield, crashed near Woking.

In 1940 the airfield defences were strengthened. Huts were built to house 150 men of the Coldstream Guards from Purbright, later replaced by the 10th Training Regiment, RA from Blackdown barracks. They took over two gun-posts with Bofors guns and later seven concrete pill-boxes were built housing Lewis guns. As defence against paratroops Fairoaks had two armoured converted army lorries, a Bedford Armadillo and a Leyland Pill Box. The airfield buildings were camouflaged and the landing area had simulated hedgerows painted on the grass with tar, which may have been disconcerting to the pupils attempting circuits and landings.

April 7th/8th saw the only air raid on the airfield. There was a particularly heavy raid during the night and 150 to 200 incendiary bombs were dropped by a lone raider on to No 2 hangar, setting fire to two Tiger Moths, a Magister and a Vega Gull. A bomb also fell on the sick quarters.

By July 1941 the number of pupils had increased further and one flight was detached to Smiths Lawn, a grass airfield in Windsor Great Park. By September Fairoaks had increased to two flights, with C flight at Winkfield and D flight at Smiths Lawn. Instructors would fly out with a pupil each morning to the satellite fields, the rest following by coach, all returning at night.

As with other airfields, Fairoaks had its share of visitors. Some were aircraft in distress, short of fuel and en route to Brooklands in bad weather, not happy negotiating the balloon barrage guarding the airfield. Wellingtons often flew in, and on one occasion one arrived to take temporary shelter from the weather but on being towed to the dispersal area sank deeply in the mud and stayed for two weeks. Wellingtons Mk V and VI – the high altitude version – sometimes flew in from Smiths Lawn where Vickers had a production line situated in a Bellman hangar. A Mosquito completely out of fuel, returning after a photo shoot over Noball sites, attempted the short runway, braked, slid and crashed into a parked Blenheim. The crew jumped out quickly, removing the camera, and were whisked away by car to finish their journey to Benson.

The employees of the airfield had organised a Wings for Victory committee and raised enough money to fund the purchase of an aeroplane. They chose a Typhoon and in recognition of their good

Sergeant Webb, RCAF, flying instructor with B flight of 18 EFTS, carrying out the daily inspection of a Tiger Moth, March 1942. (A. S. Webb)

Pilot Officers Nelles, Wood, Maunsell, Millichap, and Looin, instructional staff of B flight, 18 EFTS, in March 1942. (A. S. Webb)

work, Wing Commander R. Beamont, a great exponent of the aircraft, flew in and gave a display, to the delight of the assembled workforce.

By November 1941 the pilot shortage was becoming more acute and further measures were needed to speed up the output from the schools, so the Grading Scheme was introduced. Each course would last three weeks with a maximum of 15 hours' flying. If during the course the instructor was satisfied the pupil would go solo if allowed to continue, he was immediately sent to Hooton Park to await posting overseas as part of the Empire Training Scheme in Canada or Rhodesia. To increase output at Fairoaks, 15 instructors had 36 pupils per flight on 18 aircraft. The two flights were split into morning and afternoon, each flight accomplishing three and a half hours per day. The rest of the day was spent in ground training and lectures.

By June 1943 the school was logging over 2,000 flying hours per month and the ATC gliding school commenced flying the Kirby Cadet and Dagling primary gliders. This total had risen to over 3,600 hours in June 1944. By the next month, however, training output started to reduce and by May 1945 was finished. Flying was reduced, with

The flight hut of 18 EFTS, 1942, now the home of London Transport Flying Club. Note the petrol bowser in the foreground. (A. Milton)

refresher courses for pilots and initial training for army glider pilots on powered aircraft. After the war it diminished still further until on 14th May 1947 the EFTS was disbanded and reformed as No 18 Reserve Flying School, keeping voluntary reserve pilots up to scratch on Tiger Moths and later Chipmunks and Ansons. This too was disbanded in July 1953 along with all the other Reserve Schools.

Civil flying commenced at Fairoaks soon after the war. One of the first operators was Universal Flying Services with their Rapides on charter work, and the flying clubs of Fairoaks, Midland Bank and London Transport were soon in operation. A hard runway was laid in 1980 and today Fairoaks Airport is a busy centre for light aircraft and helicopters.

7
GATWICK

On 6th June 1936 Gatwick was reopened after completion of various improvements including the building of a new terminal, hangars and a railway station. The ceremony was followed by a flying display of civil and service aircraft. The terminal building, an innovative design by the architects Hoar, Marlow and Lovett, was three-storeyed like a Martello tower and was known affectionately as the 'Beehive'. It had six telescopic canopies radiating out like arms from the building to the waiting aircraft, ensuring that the passengers were under cover from the time of alighting from the train, via an underground tunnel connecting the station to the terminal.

Gatwick was operated by Airports Ltd and looked forward to

Gatwick airport after completion in 1936, showing the hangars, terminal building and railway station. (BAA Gatwick)

attracting airline operators. British Airways had been at Gatwick since May and was encouraged by the government to develop the European routes abandoned by Imperial Airways, in pursuit of the Empire routes. However, difficulties soon arose for BA. The fatal crash of a night mail DH 86 highlighted take-off problems, with some aircraft finding the northerly runways too short and having to use the concrete taxiway. Another fatal crash led the Air Ministry to prohibit further night flying until a Lorenz blind-flying beam was installed.

On top of this the winter of 1936 was very wet, the airfield became very muddy due to drains collapsing, and the larger, heavier Junkers 52 and Fokker Trimotors could not operate. In consequence, in 1937 British Airways moved out to Croydon. This was a severe blow to Airports Ltd but fortunately the two other airlines, Air Travel and Air Touring, continued with their lighter aircraft. However, hopes of Gatwick becoming the second London Airport were dashed when the government announced that it would be taking over Heston airport for the second London terminal.

The British Airways maintenance section continued at Gatwick and Surrey Flying services carried out some pupil training, but the real boost came in October 1937 when Airports Ltd opened No 19 E&RFTS to train volunteer reserve pilots, mainly at weekends, using the facilities of Air Travel. British Airways set up a pilot training school in the terminal, teaching the latest in blind-flying on Link trainers and Fokker Trimotors, but moved out with the maintenance section to Heston in May 1938. Fortunately the vacated BA hangar was soon occupied by Airwork Ltd who had obtained a government contract under the Civil Repair Organisation to modify Whitley bombers. On 25th June crowds flocked to see an excellent flying display at Gatwick sponsored by the *Daily Express* featuring civil and RAF aircraft and army AA units. *Flight* records that 150,000 people attended.

Later, in September 1938, Airports Ltd obtained a further contract to train direct entry officers. This required further aircraft, more instructors and one of the new Bellman hangars. The Insurance Club moved in and started a Civil Air Guard scheme and with business booming, the summer of 1939 saw the sky between Redhill and Gatwick, with only four nautical miles separation, become extremely crowded. Sadly, accidents began to happen. In May a Hart collided with a Redhill CAG Gipsy Moth and all occupants were killed, and in August a Hind, Tiger Moth and Magister crashed, all from Gatwick.

The training came to an abrupt end when war commenced. The CAG ceased to exist and No 19 E&RFTS, with aircraft and instructors, moved

The original Gatwick Airport station opened in 1936. (Lens of Sutton)

to Fairoaks on 1st September 1939. Gatwick was requisitioned and became a war station, a satellite to Kenley and ready to take over Kenley's squadrons should problems arise. RAF personnel began to arrive but with the quiet period at the beginning of the war, there was very little activity. Airwork Ltd was busy with the Whitley conversions and Southern Aircraft (Gatwick) Ltd was engaged as a sub-contractor to Vickers producing specialised aircraft parts.

With Croydon now also a war station, British Airways (freshly amalgamated with Imperial Airways to form the British Overseas Airways Corporation) had commenced some overseas civilian airline routes from Heston, but found that it was lacking in facilities and looked once again to Gatwick for a base. The government were keen on using an airport to the south of London and Shoreham had also been considered, but British Airways put aside their previous misgivings about the mud and at the beginning of 1940 began planning the move back. The problem of operating civilian airlines from a military airfield was overcome by the Air Ministry transferring control to the Civil Aviation branch with the proviso that if RAF Kenley required the airfield it had to be vacated in 24 hours.

Work began in the new year, refurbishing the terminal building and replacing floodlights removed by the RAF, all of which was well under way by February 1940. A detachment of 92 Squadron's Spitfires arrived unexpectedly from Croydon; in the process of converting from Blenheims they used Gatwick for training. Airwork Ltd were still using the hangar for continuing contracts, but as May approached aircraft began arriving from France as the German army sped across France and Belgium and airfields there became untenable.

Meanwhile, British Airways aircraft had arrived for overhaul accompanied by a large number of BOAC maintenance personnel, but by late May it became obvious that airline operations from Gatwick were not to be.

On 26th May, No 70 Bomber Wing arrived from France with its two squadrons, 18 and 53. The following day, the terminal block was taken over and British Airways and Airports Ltd had to vacate. With the situation in France and the Low Countries deteriorating fast, Gatwick was needed for military purposes and the dream of its becoming the second London air terminal was lost again – for the present. British Airways began to move back to Heston to continue to operate any civilian routes not yet affected by the German advance.

18 and 53 Squadrons left in early June and on the 14th, 57 Squadron arrived with their Blenheim IVs to carry out reconnaissance duties. Two days later 98 Squadron were expected, but the SS *Lancastria* with the ground crew on board was sunk with great loss of life. After regrouping, the remainder, with the squadron's Battles, arrived at the end of the month. Both squadrons' stay at Gatwick was short. On 3rd July, 57 left for Detling, a Coastal Command station, and later 98 left for Iceland.

The aerodrome fell quiet whilst the Battle of Britain began to rage overhead, playing host to many visiting Home Guard detachments, and squadrons of Air Defence Cadet Corps (later Air Training Corps) who came for training. They made use of the Link trainers used previously by the British Airways training school, and as a welcome relief a much needed NAAFI was installed.

The first aircraft to arrive after the quiet spell were those of 26 Army Co-operation Squadron from West Malling on 3rd September 1940. That faithful old workhorse of army co-operation, the Westland Lysander, was a high-wing, two-seat monoplane fitted with flaps and slots enabling it to operate over a wide speed range. It had very short take-off and landing capabilities, allowing it to use very small fields and strips. A Bristol Perseus XII radial engine was fitted giving it a top speed of 230 mph at 10,000 feet with a service ceiling of 26,000 feet. A fixed 'spatted' undercarriage had a short stub wing fitted which could carry small bombs, supply packages and machine guns.

26 was a battle-hardened squadron which had gone to France in 1939 with the BEF and seen active service, not returning to Lympne until May 1940. It then became engaged in the hazardous operation of dive-bombing enemy positions and dropping supplies to the beleaguered garrison at Calais, before arriving at West Malling in June. On arrival at Gatwick the officers and men were billeted at Copthorne school. The airfield would be their base for almost two years, and they were soon heavily engaged in AA calibration duties, practice dive-bombing attacks on army units, and photo shoots.

Following 26's arrival came 141 Squadron from Turnhouse with their Boulton Paul Defiants, the personnel being housed in the terminal building. The Defiant had been switched to the night fighter role following its failure as a day fighter and was now engaged against the night raiders of the London blitz. Many pilots were untrained for night operations and training, as well as night sorties, took place. They moved out to Gravesend at the beginning of October.

During September, at the height of the Battle of Britain, enemy aircraft were frequently seen over Gatwick. On the 10th, a Dornier flew low over a nearby school and was shot down by AA fire and on the 27th an Me 110 crashed into the perimeter fence and burst into flames. On the 30th, a Ju 88 crashed on the racecourse killing one crew member; three others were taken prisoner.

1st October 1940 saw the arrival of A flight of 239 (AC) Squadron led by Squadron Leader Donkin. Equipped with Lysander IIs, they firmly established the airfield's role in army co-operation duties. The squadron had been newly formed on 18th September at Hatfield from six aircraft of 16 Squadron and six from 225 Squadron and was under the command of No 4 Army Corps. They were to be at Gatwick with 26 Squadron for the next 18 months or so. Later in the month, on the 22nd, Lysander IIIs began to arrive to replace 26's aircraft and in November they flew to Barnstaple to have 20 mm cannon fitted for improved ground support capability. In December they visited Weston Zoyland to try the new guns out on the firing range.

A flight of 239 Squadron had meanwhile been kept busy. Its main task was AA calibration flights in the London area, stretching down as far as the Medway towns. An important task, as the guns were needed every night in the continuing Blitz; the Lysanders flew accurate tracks and altitudes to enable the range finder and predictor crews to practise interception and to calibrate their instruments. Several times they practised high level dive-bombing exercises on gun sites manned by the Home Guard at Tilshead.

The Lysanders of both squadrons were equipped to spray poison gas and there was always a great fear that this fearsome weapon would be used. Practice gas spraying was in fact carried out at many army and civilian sites, though its use would only ever have been sanctioned in dire emergency.

In the middle of December the airfield was once again unserviceable due to rain and mud. 239 Squadron moved out to Hatfield to take part in a signals exercise, and on the 22nd were placed under the direction of the 1st Armoured Division, giving support to No 4 Army Corps if operations allowed.

The civilian repair and manufacturing companies had been kept busy and were now expanding. Airwork Ltd continued with the conversion of Whitley bombers and Southern Aircraft were making specialised parts for Vickers and rebuilding damaged aircraft, as well as carrying out inspections of civil aircraft.

In early January 1941 four Lysanders of 239 Squadron returned from Hatfield but bad weather with snow still curtailed operations and it was the 22nd before things improved. B flight of 239 flew in to join A flight and form a complete squadron. The officers were housed at Ifield Golf Club, the airmen at Orchard End, Lowfield Heath and the HQ at Manor Farm House in Horley. The control of the airfield moved from Fighter Command to 71 Group Army Co-operation Command.

In January and February the Lysanders carried out various operations. 26 Squadron went air firing at Old Sarum, dive-bombing on army units and drogue towing, whilst 239, now completely under the 1st Armoured Division, carried out air firing at Leysdown using Detling as a base, and participated in a 1st Armoured Signals exercise and air firing at Old Sarum and Combe Bisset.

However, experiences in France with the Lysander had raised doubts that they were suitable for the offensive operations now planned for army co-operation squadrons. They had performed sterling service but their slower speed made them vulnerable to fighter attacks when used in a close support role. Aircraft were now expected to have the capability of a fighter while being able to evade attack or defend themselves against other fighters. They also had to move in quickly on tactical reconnaissance and be able to get in and out quickly when photographing was difficult and over heavily defended targets. Several alternatives were considered. All Spitfire and Hurricane production was required by Fighter Command but the American Curtiss Tomahawk single-seat fighter was available. Not quite up to the performance of the Spitfire or the Hurricane, it was still a rugged performer with a 1,090 hp Allison V-12 engine giving it a top speed of 328 mph, and armed with two .5" Colt, and four .303" machine guns.

On 20th February 1941, Squadron Leader Butler and another pilot went to Old Sarum for a conversion course for the Tomahawks, later collecting two from Southampton and taking them on to Duxford for armament trials. In the following weeks more Tomahawks arrived and Lysanders and Tomahawks flew together in many exercises for comparison – air firing at Old Sarum, gun spotting, gas spraying, message dropping, and so on. The Tomahawks practised formation flying and had a real chance to practise their air firing when three of them shot down an escaped barrage balloon. These exercises continued throughout the summer.

The airfield was expanding and a perimeter track was completed from the racecourse, which would soon be incorporated in the landing area. The white terminal building, the 'Beehive', was camouflaged and draped with rope netting and the defences were strengthened by the arrival of the 61st Light AA Regiment.

239 Squadron was now under the sole direction of the 1st Armoured Division and commenced receiving their Lysander III aircraft, which then flew to Barnstaple to have twin 20 mm cannon fitted. Several of

A Curtiss Tomahawk I of 26 Squadron, used as a replacement for the Lysander, 1941. (RAF Museum)

146

the squadron's Lysanders were sent on detachment to Coastal Command airfields employed on air-sea rescue work, and squadron mobility exercises were carried out using Advanced Landing Grounds at Old Sarum, Tilshead and Harwell. Then in May, Air Vice Marshal Maltby, AOC 71 Group, inspected the squadron and informed them that they were no longer with the 1st Armoured Division but had been taken over by the 8th Armoured Division in the Surrey area.

June 1941 saw 239's first Tomahawks arrive and Wing Commander Donkin and two other pilots went to Old Sarum for a conversion course. Exercises continued with the new Tomahawks alongside the Lysanders for the 8th Armoured Division and the Canadian Army, consisting of low level bombing using the Lydd range, night flying, air-to-air and air-to-ground communications with the new VHF radio sets, and tactical reconnaissance. Two Lysanders collided at Shepherdswell during this period.

In August No 71 Group, Army Co-operation Command was disbanded in favour of more local Army Co-operation Wings. No 35 Wing was formed at Gatwick with its headquarters at Reigate, taking over command of 26 and 239 Squadrons and incorporating 414 Squadron based at Croydon, to serve the Army's South Eastern Command.

By September the airfield improvements had been completed. The racecourse had finally been requisitioned and two runways of army track had been laid. The main runway had been extended into the racecourse area by 350 yards and was now 1,400 yards long by 50 yards wide. Beside the two original British Airways hangars there were six Blister and one Bellman hangars and several Nissen huts. Storage capacity was 12,500 gallons of petrol, 4,000 20 lb bombs and 1,500,000 rounds of ammunition. Further strengthening of the defences had taken place when an AA battery of four 3.7" guns and eight Bofors guns were stationed near to Manor Farm at Horley. Gatwick also had a decoy airfield, a 'Q' site, situated at Lower Beeding.

After so many exercises, both squadrons were ready to commence offensive operations. On the 19th, Wing Commander P. L. Donkin and Flight Lieutenant Veal of 239 Squadron took off in their Tomahawks from their forward base at Manston, crossing the Belgian coast at Dixmude in cloud and letting down to '0' feet at Ostende. Passing Steame aerodrome they noted a runway under construction and after firing two bursts of machine gun fire at buildings across the main runway, continued along Ostende beach and dunes taking photographs as far as Dixmude. No fortifications were seen, only some barbed wire, and another short burst of gunfire damaged a gasometer at Mariankirke. The aircraft piloted by Veal flew close to Steame aerodrome and noted three large concrete gun posts nearby on the coast. Both aircraft climbed into thick cloud at 3,000 feet and returned to Gatwick via Manston. A further Rhubarb was carried out the next day before the weather became unsuitable for these type of operations.

Exercises continued, air firing into the sea off Beachy Head, and then 239 went to Netheravon on 26th September to establish an Advanced Landing Ground at Hampstead Norris, as part of Exercise Bumper. A Tomahawk crashed during the exercise and another force-landed on 2nd October at Croughton due to engine seizure. Later in the month two further accidents occurred, one due to an elevator falling off and the other to engine seizure. The lack of serviceable aircraft, particularly with 239 Squadron, was now a serious problem restricting their operations and an investigation into the failure of the Allison engines was given top priority.

On 16th October 1941, 26 Squadron opened their account with a Rhubarb, after flying down to Manston. The first sortie of 40 minutes was led by the commanding officer, Wing Commander Butler, with Pilot Officer Fleming as No 2. Flying low over the sea, they made the French coast at Le Touquet and continued a photo-reconnaissance of the beaches past Berck where they encountered heavy flak. Both Tomahawks returned safely. Meanwhile, 239 resumed operations with a Rhubarb intended to provide photo-reconnaissance of beaches from Nieuport to Dunkirk. Although flying at sea level, they were attacked by accurate flak from the ground and from ships and in this case the sortie was called off.

The next day Butler and Fleming repeated the sortie and were followed by Flight Lieutenant Goodall and Pilot Officer Bond who set out at low level to Le Tarpel. At Berck the aircraft turned north and opened fire on a gun position, scattering the crew, then turned out to sea and recrossed the coast at Merlimont Plage. They attacked troops entering a hotel at Berck, and finding little activity on the airfield continued on to a wooded area nearby where huts, lorries and troops were attacked. Another sortie, flown by Flying Officers Rhind and Donson crossed the coast three miles south of Le Touquet at '0' feet and immediately attacked a goods train, scoring hits on the wagons. The aircraft split up, one attacking a staff car and a searchlight post on the river L'Authie, while the other attacked a machine gun post on the river bank.

On 19th October, both squadrons flew Rhubarb sorties via Manston. Squadron Leader Hadfield and Flying Officer Bluett of 26 Squadron attacked the airfield at Valery St Aubin, where fire was seen to start in the hangars. They moved on to a railway siding where goods wagons were attacked. Light flak was encountered and evasive action taken by flying under power cables! On the way home three light AA posts were attacked.

From 239 Squadron, Squadron Leader Yorke and Pilot Officer Cooke flew from Manston to cross the coast at Coxyde Bains, photographing the coastline as far as Nieuport. Heavy flak was encountered, and areas covered with camouflage were noted before turning for home.

These attacks set the pattern for the coming months. Low level sea crossings were made in bad weather, by aircraft mainly in pairs, searching the beaches and coastal areas for gun emplacements, barbed wire, obstructions, invasion barges etc. Photographs were taken for the invasion planners, mainly oblique shots from cameras mounted in the fuselage behind the pilot. Crossing the coast at '0' feet, flat out, and attacking targets of opportunity that presented themselves, each sortie lasted about an hour.

While 26 Squadron continued Rhubarbs and photo-reconnaissance as the weather allowed, 239 had to restrict operations. A specialist civilian team from Burtonwood spent most of December inspecting all the Allison engines of the Tomahawks. To compensate for the lack of serviceable aircraft, in January 239 were to convert to Hurricane IIcs. Meanwhile, six Hurricanes and two Miles Master trainers were allotted, with the pilots going to Acklington for a two week conversion course.

In November, 26 took part in a different type of operation. Codenamed Arty/R, they were spotting for two 14" guns mounted on concrete bases overlooking the Channel at St Margaret's at Cliffe. The guns, known locally as *Winnie* and *Pooh*, were operated by the Royal Marine Siege Regiment and were capable of propelling a shell weighing 1,250 lbs a distance of $27\frac{1}{4}$ miles. On this occasion they were shelling the airfield across the Channel at St Inglevert. On the 6th, Wing Commander Butler took off escorted by two other Tomahawks, protected by a cover of Spitfires from 452, 485 and 602 Squadrons. On arrival over the airfield, shells were spotted falling on and around the target and he commenced plotting the positions, sending the map grid references back to the control room by radio. Cloud cover soon hampered the operation and it had to be abandoned. On the return Butler was attacked by an Me 109 but managed to take evasive action.

In January 1942, 26 were engaged in offensive photo-shoots in the Le Touquet, Etaples, Boulogne and Neufchatel areas. One Tomahawk was shot down into the sea but the pilot was picked up. The next month the airfield at Gatwick was unserviceable, but on 10th February it did open to receive replacement North American Mustang Is. These superb fighters had the more powerful Allison V-1710-39 engine of 1,150 hp with a top speed of 390 mph. Armed with four .5" and four .303" machine guns, it was ideally suited to the low and medium altitude operations carried out in Army Co-operation. During the coming months the squadron continued training and taking part in exercises with the Mustangs, Tomahawks, Lysanders and Fairey Battles.

By April 1942, 239's Tomahawks were back up to strength and operations were restarted. On the 24th, Pilot Officers King and Frampton carried out a Popular to photograph an ammunition dump at Bois de Tillegoem, five miles south of Bruges. Crossing the coast at Coxyde on their way to the target, they carried out a low level attack on a goods train moving south on a single track at Adinkirke. On returning to Coxyde after completing their mission they attacked hangars on the aerodrome and encountered five Fw 190s at 500 feet. Climbing quickly into cloud they returned to base.

On the 29th, Wing Commander Donkin carried out a night Popular, a general reconnaissance of the Nieuport-Dunkirk-Zuydcoole area at 10,000 feet. Searchlights, flak and bomb bursts were seen to the east. Ground signals were observed and going down for a closer look, he attacked a car and then a train which returned his fire with tracer from an automatic gun mounted on the tender.

In early May, 239 went to Abbottsinch for a three day combined operations course and later, on the 9th, returned there to collect ten Mustang Is and stay for a conversion course. On their return they took part in Operation Tiger from Detling, joined by detachments of 400 Squadron from Odiham and 414 from Croydon, all units living under canvas. During the exercise a Mustang from 239 flew into a hill four miles west of Maidstone. Whilst the squadrons were away, 171 Squadron, with Tomahawks, was formed at Gatwick.

In the coming months the offensive operations of the two squadrons increased. Airfields, railways, communications, and invasion barges in the Pas de Calais were attacked and photographed indicating the Allies were working up to something big. VHF radios were now fitted to all aircraft. On 19th August 1942, the Allies returned to France in the first combined operation, Operation Jubilee, a raid on the town of Dieppe. The two squadrons, joined by 400 and 414, again operated under No 35 Wing and were given the task of tactical reconnaissance of roads, communications and troop movements in the surrounding area. Two plane sorties were flown, the first by two Mustangs of 239. They were airborne at 4.30 am, flown by the commanding officer, Wing Commander Donkin and Pilot Officer Green, and reported much activity over Dieppe.

Over the next seven hours 26 Squadron flew eleven sorties, their first at 8.30 am, and 239 flew 14 sorties. 26 flew in the Le Havre, Rouen, Abbeville and mouth of the Somme areas reporting on transport and troop movements and attacking ground targets, while 239 flew low tactical reconnaissance of roads from Le Tréport to Envernay and Blancy. On one sortie west of Dieppe, there was flak and the two Mustangs were attacked by four Fw 190s. On another, Squadron Leader McLean's Mustang was hit by flak, damaging oil pipes and forcing him to land at Friston. Flight Lieutenant Bonn on the Yerville, Rouen and Yvetot area reconnaissance was attacked by four Fw 190s. Shaking off the attack he hit one of them, which was then finished by a friendly Spitfire, both pilots claiming a half. The last sortie was flown by 400 Squadron at 1.15 pm. It had been a hard day, 26 Squadron losing five pilots and aircraft and 239, three pilots and aircraft. The next day the Air Officer Commander in Chief of No 71 Group, Sir Arthur Barrett, visited the airfield and spoke to pilots.

On 30th August 1942, after a stay of almost two years, 239 Squadron with nine Mustangs, a Tomahawk, a Battle and a Tiger Moth left for Twinwood Farm, although some of the aircraft continued to use the airfield for a few weeks. August also saw the return of 171 Squadron with their Tomahawks, which were replaced by Mustangs in September. The next month they commenced operations, photo-reconnaissance and interceptor patrols, but left for Hartfordbridge in December.

The closing months of 1942 saw detachments of various squadrons arrive for operational experience. 175 Squadron with their Hurricane IIcs replaced 171, the squadron converting from Fighter Command to Army Co-operation. Others to arrive were B flight of 309 (Polish) Squadron from Dalcross and C flight of 4 Squadron from York. After the Dieppe operation, 26 Squadron continued to operate interceptor patrols along the south coast before returning to Rhubarbs and Populars and photo-reconnaissance. The squadron continued at Gatwick until January 1943 when they moved, after a stay of two years and three months, to Detling. At the end of the year, Penshurst was made a satellite of Gatwick.

The new year of 1943 started wet and there was little activity, the airfield being unserviceable except for light aircraft. In March things

The Hawker Typhoon Ibs of 183 Squadron, April 1943. The racecourse and old grandstand can be seen in the background. (Imperial War Museum)

improved and on the 7th, in connection with the formation of the 2nd Tactical Air Force, 26 and 239 Squadrons returned as part of No 123 Airfield. On the 9th, 183 Squadron with its Typhoon Ibs arrived to make up the full complement. In keeping with the policy of the 2nd TAF the airfield was accommodated under canvas and there was much scrounging for tents and camping equipment, everyone being thankful that the weather was fine.

The two Mustang squadrons now embarked on an intensive period of training with new techniques and in operating with the other services, whilst the Typhoons familiarised themselves with the area by flying standing patrols. The Typhoon was new to Gatwick. Designed as an interceptor, its performance was found to be disappointing at high altitude but at low altitude it performed well. Fitted with the Napier Sabre engine of 2,100 to 2,260 hp, it could reach 412 mph at 19,000 feet and was found to be a very stable gun platform, its four 20 mm Hispano cannon able to be fired with great accuracy. It could also carry up to 2,000 lb of bombs and when fitted with up to eight 60 lb rockets became devastating as a ground attack weapon.

On 17th April, 183 Squadron flew down to Ford on the Sussex coast for their first bombing mission. Bad weather delayed the operation until the 19th when four Typhoons loaded with 500 lb bombs ('Bomphoons') escorted by four Typhoons with cannon took off to attack the power station at Yainville. On the way they picked up their escort, the Canadian wing led by Wing Commander 'Johnnie' Johnson with their Spitfire IXs from Kenley. On arrival at the target there was full cloud cover and slipping below this from the east, the four Typhoons sped low across to their target, dropping their bombs and away, to be followed by the escorting Typhoons who attacked the target with cannon. Withdrawing at ground level, Flight Lieutenant Bridge and Flying Officer Gottow attacked a train and an army lorry, all aircraft returning safely. The next day they took part in Operation Curley Kale 'attacking' army lorries, troops and AA sites near Cowes and after a cancelled shipping strike from Exeter, the squadron left Gatwick on 3rd May for Lasham.

On 1st June 1943, with the disbanding of the Army Co-operation Command, it being absorbed into the 2nd TAF, RAF Gatwick was transferred to 11 Group, Fighter Command and was now under the control of Kenley. Also associated with the 2nd TAF at Gatwick was No 403 Repair and Service Unit. No 2773 RAF Regiment arrived and merged with No 4155 AA Flight to be responsible, with the Home Guard, for airfield defence.

On 21st June, 26 and 239 Squadrons moved to Odiham, followed two days later by No 123 Airfield HQ and later by No 35 Wing. On 5th July Gatwick welcomed the Canadian 414 and 430 Squadrons to form No 129 Airfield, who after Dunsfold found Gatwick small and bumpy. It did not help that the weather was bad and pilots and airmen under canvas were occupied digging trenches around their tents to improve the drainage!

414 Squadron were soon busy with training and army exercises, plus many photo-shoots and night flying. On 30th July they flew with a Typhoon squadron bombing Poix aerodrome as a photo-exercise, catching the bomb bursts on film. 430 were also training and flew some Rhubarbs and Populars. On 7th August, the Mustangs moved to Attlebridge to take part in an army exercise, returning on the 11th before both squadrons moved out to the Advanced Landing Ground at Ashford, leaving Gatwick without a resident squadron.

The airfield was reduced to a care and maintenance status but not without a continuous stream of aircraft landing, some lost, some damaged and often with wounded on board, some short of fuel. Halifaxes, Lancasters, Whitleys, Thunderbolts and Fortresses were regular visitors. One Fortress landed, skidded and crashed into a parked Halifax, badly damaging both aircraft. The constant pounding by these heavy aircraft damaged the runways and Sommerfeld tracking was used to repair them. To assist these aircraft in finding their way Gatwick had a Darky homing beacon installed.

In August No 84 Group Communications flight moved in from Cowley for a six-month stay, and on 15th October Gatwick became operational again. No 129 Airfield moved back from Ashford ALG but now comprised 430 Squadron with Mustangs and 65 and 122 Squadrons with Spitfire IXs, to be joined by another Spitfire IX squadron, 19 from Weston Zoyland. 122 soon left for Weston Zoyland leaving the other Spitfire squadron on bomber escort duties until they left for Gravesend on the 24th. This coincided with early heavy rains. Contractors were called in to drain the airfield and later on the two main runways were closed except for operational aircraft.

On 3rd November, 414 Squadron flew in from Redhill to join 430 to operate as No 129 Airfield under No 39 Reconnaissance Wing (Redhill) and next day attempted a photo-reconnaissance of the Channel Islands. This was followed on the 5th by a Ranger in the south Holland area when a Ju 52 was destroyed on the ground and trains and power lines were hit. The commanding officer of 414, Squadron Leader Peters attacked a small barge in heavy flak, when his Mustang was hit and caught fire. Attempting to land in the mud he jettisoned the hood but the aircraft crashed and he was, tragically, killed. One other aircraft and pilot were lost.

At the end of the year the airfield was still unserviceable, the runways used by operational aircraft only, and contractors were still employed on drainage work. To ease the situation 430 Squadron flew up to No 15 Armament Practice Camp at Peterhead early in January 1944, followed later by 414, to practise spotting for naval guns, both returning on the 23rd. They practised local flying for a while, before leaving again in early February, 414 to Peterhead and 430 to York. With the squadrons away an airfield defence exercise was held with the Home Guard attacking, supported by aircraft from Redhill. By the end of February 414 and 430 had returned, to be joined in early March by 168 Fighter Reconnaissance Squadron with their Mustang IAs, who would complement No 129 Airfield when photographing specialist targets. Up to now, target priority had been given to railways and marshalling yards but it now switched to the secret weapon sites that had been discovered in northern France.

By this time the order of battle was being drafted for the coming

Mustangs of 2 Squadron, up from Gatwick 1944. (MAP)

invasion, with forces and squadrons settling down at the bases they would occupy when operations began. Gatwick was now transferred from the Kenley sector to Biggin Hill. At the end of March, No 129 Airfield (168, 414 and 430 Squadrons) moved to Odiham along with No 39 Wing who established there. 660 AOP Squadron (84 Group) with its Austers would now fly in to Gatwick to practise night flying. The seven AOP squadrons chosen as part of the 2nd TAF practised night flying at various bases in case they were required to cross the Channel in darkness following the invasion forces. Handley Page Harrow transports also visited the airfield to demonstrate the handling of casualties when they were used as air ambulances.

In April, No 130 Airfield, with 2, 4 and 268 Squadrons, moved in from Sawbridgeworth, setting up its own flying control to operate under field conditions. They now came under No 35 Reconnaissance Wing which also moved in and set up its HQ. 2 and 268 Squadrons were equipped with Mustangs for tactical reconnaissance and 4 Squadron with Spitfire IXs and Mosquito IVs for photo-reconnaissance. The three squadrons were soon busy on operations but the Mosquitos were finding the 1,400 yard length of the main runway a little tight and were later exchanged for Spitfires.

The commanding officer of No 35 Wing was Group Captain P. L. Donkin, no stranger to Gatwick, who flew on a tactical 'recce' in a 268

The faithful 'Annie', the Avro Anson used at Gatwick on many duties including communications, ferrying, ambulances and radar calibration. (C. Nepean Bishop)

Squadron Mustang. After completing a photographic run his aircraft was hit by flak. He successfully baled out over the sea and made for a dinghy. The radio of his No 2 had failed and his position could not be radioed to base. Despite a concerted air-sea rescue operation he drifted for six days before he was finally picked up off Dover.

4 Squadron were employed photographing at high level areas in Belgium and northern France right up to the invasion. When D-Day arrived the cloud cover was solid over the landing areas and the squadron log records it as 'the most disappointing day in their history'. Only one sortie was flown. The Mustang squadrons, however, were engaged in spotting for the naval bombardment. Low level photo-reconnaissance of road and rail movements took place under heavy flak conditions and several aircraft were lost. It was six days before the weather cleared and 4 Squadron could fly their high level sorties, with 22 flown over the Seine-Mezidon area. Two days later they managed 23 from Dieppe to Rouen. The three squadrons continued operations until 27th June 1944 and with the sense of a job well done, No 130 Airfield moved to Odiham.

On the same day 80, 229 and 274 Air Defence of Great Britain Squadrons arrived from Merston with their Spitfire IXs. They were engaged upon fighter sweeps and escorting bombers until July when the V1 rockets appeared and the squadrons moved out. On 1st July the RAF Regiment at Gatwick shot down their first V1 and by the 9th, barrage balloons began to appear around the airfield.

Gatwick was for a time non-operational but in August 116 Squadron's Ansons and Oxfords arrived on AA calibration and stayed for a week before moving to Redhill. 236 Air Co-operation Squadron with Hurricanes, Oxfords, some Spitfires and Typhoons, stayed for four months before it too moved to Redhill; No 49 Maintenance Unit was on hand to service the many types of aircraft using the airfield. As the Allied advance across Europe continued, Gatwick saw a great deal of traffic movement. Ansons, Oxfords and Dakotas took officers to Normandy and by September, air ambulances were beginning to arrive with casualties. By October the Dakotas of the Canadian Casualty Evacuation Unit were using Gatwick, transferring the wounded to their hospital at Smallfield.

Unfortunately, by December the airfield was flooded again; the courier service to Europe moved to Northolt and by the end of January 1945 the Canadian Casualty Evacuation Unit had moved to Redhill. The airfield closed on a care and maintenance basis and became a satellite of Biggin Hill on 1st February.

Gatwick was now home to 1337 Wing of SHAEF but in a few days was taken over by a SHAEF disarmament unit, also on a lodger basis, and part of No 1337 RAF Regiment. The airfield was soon waterlogged again but in March was serviceable enough for No 85 Group Communications Flight to move in and operate their Ansons flying VIPs to the continent. In May, with the war in Europe over, the airfield transferred from Biggin Hill to become a satellite of Dunsfold, until August when it was taken over by No 103 Air Disarmament Wing, the SHAEF unit moving out to the Continent.

Gatwick now became extremely busy with all types of aircraft arriving and 49 MU busy servicing Mosquitos. By October it was becoming quieter but was still responsible for providing transport for BAFO personnel to and from Europe. By this time 85 GCS had been joined by 84 and 83 GCS. Servicing at the airfield increased as 49 MU was now looking after all the Group Communications aircraft. By January 1946 they were servicing 16 aircraft per day, but the airfield itself continued to be run down and by February had become a diversion for West Malling. By 31st August only the civil repair organisations (Airwork repairing Wellingtons and Southern Aircraft repairing Beaufighters), one BAFO aircraft and the Ministry of Civil Aviation who controlled the airfield remained. All other personnel had departed.

The future of Gatwick was now uncertain. In 1943 Airports Ltd's managing director, Mr M. Desoutter, in a visionary venture had commissioned the aviation consultants Messrs Norman and Dawborn to produce a feasibility study for a post-war Gatwick and two schemes were put forward. It was realised that long distance air travel with large airliners would require extensive landing grounds and that London would need more than one airport. Gatwick, to the south of London, was that much nearer to the Continent and with a high speed rail link to the capital was an ideal site for a major airport.

The consultants' 'small' scheme suggested an increase of size to 500 acres with four hard runways, 1,400 to 1,800 metres long, without disturbing the racecourse or the river Mole. In the 'large' scheme, developing Gatwick into an international airport demanded absorbing the racecourse, diverting the river Mole and providing six runways of 1,300 to 2,300 metres in length.

The Government, however, had earmarked Heathrow as the London airport; Gatwick did not figure in its plans and indeed, they were prepared to sell it off as part of the Crawley new town development. However, Desoutter persuaded the Government there was a need for an airport catering for the rapidly expanding charter airline market and a licence for scheduled passenger flying was granted to Gatwick in November 1946. Business progressed steadily but in 1948 Airports Ltd were advised by the Ministry of Civil Aviation, who still controlled the airport under the wartime powers, of the Government's intention to derequisition the airport in September 1949 and develop Stanstead as a diversionary airport.

In 1949 the future of Gatwick was saved by Mr Peter Masefield (later, Sir Peter Masefield), at that time Chief Executive of British European Airways, requesting that Gatwick be chosen rather than Stanstead for the diversionary airport. He could see that by 1955 Heathrow would not be able to handle BEA's number of flights to the Continent when they had to leave Northolt. Gatwick was nearer to the Continent and had a fast rail link to the city. In 1952 the Government, after much deliberation, announced that Gatwick would become the second airport to Heathrow, and after settling many disputes, work began in 1956 on the new airport much along the lines formulated in 1943. Gatwick airport was opened on 30th May 1958, and officially opened by HM The Queen on 9th June 1958.

In its first year the airport handled 186,000 passengers, the numbers rising steadily to over 22 million in 1995. It is expected to reach 30 million by the turn of the century.

8
BROOKLANDS

Brooklands, the birthplace of British aviation, was unique in that it started life as an internationally famous motor racing circuit and finished as an equally famous aerodrome and aircraft production centre. By the 1930s it had recovered from the ravages of the First World War and could claim to be in its golden era. Motor racing was in full swing and at weekends crowds flocked to the track to be thrilled by such names as Malcolm Campbell (later Sir Malcolm), Major H. Segrave (later Sir Henry), George Eyston, Raymond Mays and many

Vickers production sheds between the wars. (Vickers plc)

others racing their cars around the banked track.

In the centre of the pear-shaped track was a grass flying area where the various activities co-existed harmoniously with the motor racing. There were air displays, the finishing leg of the King's Cup was held there several times, and many well known civilian pilots kept their aircraft at Brooklands. The Brooklands School of Flying, started in 1928 by Capt Duncan Davies, gave instruction and the Brooklands Flying Club was founded soon afterwards, both counting amongst their members a number of famous personalities, royalty, and stars of stage and screen. Brooklands was the place to be!

Vickers Aircraft Ltd in 1932 rebuilt their manufacturing site on the eastern side of the aerodrome, on the site of the old Itala motor works. They also occupied one block of the old 1917 Belfast hangars as test sheds, next door to the dreaded sewage farm. Hawkers were manufacturing their aircraft at their works in Kingston and transporting them to Brooklands for test flying. They occupied another block of Belfast hangars and in 1934 built a long erection shed on the site of the original hangars.

The third and centre block of hangars was occupied by Brooklands Flying School and Club, in front of which was built a distinctive clubhouse and control tower.

In the early 1930s Vickers were producing the Virginia bomber, the Victoria and Valentia biplane transports, and the Vildebeeste torpedo bomber. Hawkers were busy building and test flying their successful range of variants based on the Hart and culminating in the beautiful and fast Fury. But it was all about to change, for aircraft design was in a new and exciting era. Sydney Camm (later Sir Sydney Camm), chief designer of Hawkers, realised that the successful biplane design had reached the end of its life if higher speeds were required and so channelled his skills into monoplane fighter design. Vickers meanwhile, with the end of their venture into airship design in 1930 and the liquidation of the Airship Guarantee Company, invited N. B. Wallis (later Sir Barnes Wallis) to join them as chief structures designer at Weybridge alongside R. Pierson, chief designer. Barnes Wallis brought fresh ideas to the design of aircraft based on knowledge gained in the use of light alloys in airship design.

In 1932 Vickers tendered for specification M1/60, a biplane torpedo bomber embodying light alloy in its construction, and the prototype was flown by Joseph 'Mutt' Summers, Vickers' chief test pilot, with J. Radcliffe as observer in 1933. However, it broke up in mid air during a dive. Both occupants were thrown out but parachuted to safety.

Vickers also tendered for specification 04/31 which called for a general purpose bomber/torpedo biplane. They put forward three designs, two of which were for monoplanes. The Air Ministry decided to adopt the well tried biplane design, which had a fuselage built of aluminium alloy giving a much lighter aeroplane. Meanwhile, as a private venture, Vickers had proceeded with a monoplane design, the fuselage and wings constructed to a new design by Wallis whereby the alloy members followed geodetic curves to form a lattice framework, giving a very strong and light structure. When flown against the biplane, the monoplane showed such improved performance in speed and load carrying that the order for the biplane was cancelled.

In September 1935 a new specification for a monoplane was issued, to be named the Wellesley. It had a single Bristol Pegasus X engine, a high aspect ratio wing span of 74 feet and a top speed of 213 mph. The first production Wellesley was flown by 'Mutt' Summers on 30th January 1937 and by 1938 four squadrons had received their new machines in the UK and three overseas. The design of the Wellesley made it admirably suited to long range work and on 5th November

Wellington production, a fine example of the basket weave geodetic construction designed by Barnes Wallis, 1939. (Vickers plc)

Prototype Wellington Mk I, L 4212, being rolled across the river Wey from the production sheds to the flying area. (Vickers plc)

1938, Squadron Leader Kellet led a flight of three Wellesleys non-stop from Ismalia in Egypt to Darwin in Australia, a distance of 7,157.7 miles in 48 hours, the record standing for eight years.

In parallel with the Wellesley production was the development of a bomber to specification B9/32, issued in October 1932. This was to become one of the most famous wartime aircraft and be produced in far greater numbers than any other bomber. Advances in the design of aircraft were happening so fast that the Air Ministry specifications were unrealistic and Vickers and other manufacturers persuaded them that the new aircraft should have the most powerful engines available. The prototype was based on a full geodetic design using knowledge gained from the Wellesley development, and fitted with two Bristol Pegasus X engines of 915 hp with a medium wing and two power-operated turrets. The prototype Wellington flew on 15th June 1936 at Brooklands, piloted by 'Mutt' Summers with Barnes Wallis on board, and by 1937 it was in squadron service.

Concurrent with the development of the Wellington was that of the lesser known Warwick. Both aircraft were developed together and

162

were distinctly similar in appearance. The Warwick was bigger overall but many of the structural units were the same for both aircraft. It was being developed as a heavy bomber using the new generation of more powerful engines that were promised but development was delayed due to problems with these engines.

Hawker Aircraft Ltd (formerly HG Hawker Engineering Co Ltd) in the 1930s were very busy at their Canbury Park Road works in Kingston producing their most successful design, the Hart and its many variants – the Demon, Hind, Audax, culminating in the Fury biplane fighter. All were erected and test flown at Brooklands. By 1933 Hawkers had put forward a monoplane fighter design based on the Fury by Sydney Camm with the new Rolls-Royce Merlin engine. An order was placed in February 1935 for a prototype and by the 23rd October the fuselage and wings had been transported from Kingston, under wraps, to Brooklands where they were erected under the watchful eye of P. W. S. Bulman, chief test pilot of Hawkers.

On 6th November 1935 the slight, balding figure of Bulman climbed into the cockpit of K 5083, took off and flew the first British aeroplane capable of over 300 mph. After some teething troubles, mainly with the engine, Bulman delivered the Hurricane to Martlesham for certification where it achieved 315 mph at 16,000 feet. Hawkers did not wait for government contracts but went ahead at Kingston with plans for the production of a thousand aircraft. Erection was carried out at Brooklands in a new shed on the site of the old original sheds. By September 1939 there were 18 Hurricane squadrons in service.

Brooklands was also associated with the development of the Spitfire. In 1928 Vickers Ltd purchased the Supermarine Aviation works at Woolston, famous for its Schneider Trophy seaplanes designed by R. J. Mitchell. The company was a wholly owned subsidiary and although its works would operate independently of Vickers Aircraft at Weybridge, all test flying would be carried out by and be the responsibility of the test department at Weybridge under 'Mutt' Summers, Vickers' chief test pilot.

R. J. Mitchell, the chief designer of Supermarine, was working on a design specification F37/34 for a single-engined, eight-gun fighter and by 1935, after several design attempts, arrived at a satisfactory solution. A prototype (K5054) was made at Woolston, transported to Eastleigh and test flown by Summers on 6th March 1936. Pilot Officer Jeffrey Quill AFC, another Vickers test pilot and assistant to Summers, witnessed the flight and records in *Birth of a Legend* that the flight was satisfactory and that after landing Summers said, 'I don't want

163

Group Captain P. W. S. ('George') Bulman MC, AFC, chief Hawker test pilot.
(Brooklands Museum)

164

The Hawker Hurricane prototype, first flown by George Bulman in front of the Belfast hangar, Hawkers flight shed. (R. Riding)

anything touched'. This remark was to become widely misinterpreted, but what he meant was that there were no snags requiring attention.

Afterwards Quill flew Summers back to Brooklands in the company's Miles Falcon Six. Pleased with the success of the first flight of the Spitfire prototype they stopped for a drink in the Brooklands' flying club bar and realised that not a hundred yards away in the hangar was the prototype that Bulman had flown four months earlier. They did not, of course, appreciate at the time that in four years both aircraft would be needed to save Britain in the biggest air battle ever known.

Jeffrey Quill, along with George Pickering, a Supermarine test pilot, carried out the development test flying of the Spitfire in between testing Wellesleys and Wellingtons, flying down to Eastleigh by day in the Falcon as required. He moved to Supermarine permanently in 1938, and rejoined the RAF during the Battle of Britain, testing Spitfires under battle conditions.

When war commenced all motor racing and civil flying at Brooklands ceased. Vickers were concentrating on the production of the Wellington. Production of the Wellesley had ceased; of the 176

Joseph 'Mutt' Summers, chief test pilot of Vickers. He joined them in 1928 from the RAF and A.E.& E., Martlesham Heath. When he retired in 1951, he had flown over thirty prototypes including the Spitfire, Wellington, Warwick, Viscount and Valiant. (Brooklands Museum)

Wellesleys made, four UK squadrons were equipped with them and three in the Middle East. The first Wellington to enter squadron service went to 99 Squadron in October 1938, and replacement continued until by the time war was declared ten squadrons had been re-equipped, replacing Heyfords, Harrows, a few Hendons and the Wellesleys, although the latter continued their service in the Middle East.

The 'Wimpy', as it was affectionately known by bomber crews, continued its development during the war using a variety of engines, sometimes dictated by availability, and was adapted to perform many duties, one of which was the carrying of the 4,000 lb bomb. In mid 1940 Barnes Wallis modified a Wellington Mk II to house the 'cookie' by removing the intermediate bomb doors and fixing strengthening beams. This proved successful and these Wellington conversions were known as Type 423.

At the end of August and beginning of September 1940, with the Battle raging overhead, several bombs fell in the vicinity of the works during day and night raids. Then, on Wednesday 4th September, Brooklands was the subject of a savage and surprise air attack. An enemy raid had built up over southern England at midday and though it was being monitored its exact target had not been established. A smaller raid was also noticed crossing the coast but was lost, and thought to have merged with the larger raid. At 1.12 pm, the official report at the time states, six Me 110s dived from the east-northeast and six Ju 88s from the south-southeast, from 25,000 feet down to 500 feet, missing the balloon barrage. They dropped their bombs on the heavily camouflaged Vickers works, afterwards climbing away to the north-west. Later reports suggest approximately 20 aircraft took part.

It was lunch time and some people were sitting in the sun outside but most were still in the canteen which received the full blast of the first bomb to fall. Many were killed and most sustained injuries from flying debris and bomb splinters. Several more people were killed when a bomb fell on the machine shop where they were waiting to clock on after the lunch break. The bombs fell without warning, everyone taken by complete surprise without time to take cover, the havoc being wrought by twelve 500 kg and twelve 250 kg bombs. As the raiders sped away, the AA guns opened up and two aircraft were thought to have been hit. Overhead 253 Squadron Hurricanes, patrolling nearby, pounced on them and accounted for more.

The raid was savage and the casualties heavy. Seventy five men and five women were killed, 176 seriously injured and 243 slightly injured. Four unidentified bodies were buried in Burvale Cemetery.

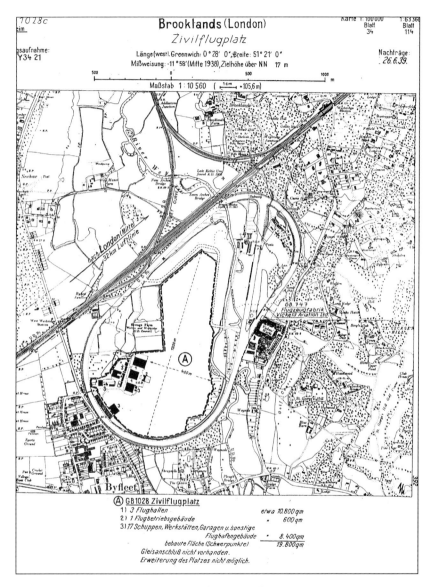

A German target map of Brooklands airfield. (C. Elliott)

Night raids continued in the area but no further bombs fell on Brooklands. The main damage was to the machine shop, electrical wiring department and the repair hangar. Whilst the damage was being sorted out, a great deal of work was taken on by sub contractors in the area. Wellington production was held up for 22 hours but Hawkers, fortunately, were unaffected.

Hawkers had been busy since before the war started erecting and flying the Hurricane manufactured at their Kingston works. They had tendered for a two-seat light bomber, closely related to the Hurricane and named the Henley, which first flew in 1937 from Brooklands. It never fulfilled the role of bomber, however, and it spent the war as a target tug, produced at Gloster's. Hawker Aircraft also produced one prototype two-seat interceptor, the Hotspur, which first flew in 1938, but this lost out to the Boulton Paul Defiant and was also dropped.

However, in 1937, Sydney Camm had two fighters on the Hawker drawing board to succeed the Hurricane when more powerful engines became available. The first to fly was the Tornado in October 1939, powered with the ill fated Rolls-Royce Vulture engine. A second prototype was flown but further trouble with the engine caused development to be suspended. The second fighter design to fly was the Typhoon on 24th February 1940, powered with the Napier Sabre 2,100 hp engine. This proved to be successful and the genesis of a new

A Hurricane IIc armed with four 20 mm cannon, 1942. Note Wellingtons in the background and the protective curtain of barrage balloons. (Brooklands Museum)

line of piston-engined fighters, but was unfortunately the last new Hawker design to be tested at Brooklands, all future development transferring to their aerodrome at Langley. Hurricane production continued at Brooklands until 1942 when it also moved to Langley.

In 1942 Barnes Wallis's genius for aerodynamics was switched to the design of bombs. Bigger bombs were required to penetrate more heavily constructed targets – the 100 foot thick walls of dams, or the reinforced concrete submarine pens or underground munition works often sited in deep caves in the side of hills. Amongst the designs were the ten-ton 'Grand Slam' and the streamlined 12,000 lb 'Tall Boy' with offset fins to promote spinning to assist penetration before exploding. The first successful use of the Tall Boy was against the battleship *Tirpitz*, dropped by Lancasters; one scored a direct hit, badly disabling her.

But Barnes Wallis's most famous design was the 'Bouncing Bomb'. He had long held the belief that if the giant dams holding water for the hydro-electric power stations serving the industrial and munitions factories in the Ruhr valley could be breached, the subsequent flooding would neutralise many of the factories and so cripple the German war effort. Normal bombing, even with Tall Boys, would not work and the inner walls of the dams were protected from torpedoes by steel nets. His idea was to drop a bomb, allow it to bounce on the water and finally sink at the dam face to explode at a predetermined depth. It was similar to the effect of skimming a stone across a pond and seeing it bounce a few times before finally sinking. Simple in principle but almost impossible to translate into practical terms.

After initial stiff opposition to his scheme, Barnes Wallis was finally given the go ahead to produce the bomb. Designing at home and experimenting with a catapult and marbles in long tanks of water at Teddington to obtain data, a prototype bomb was produced at Brooklands. A faithful Wellington was modified to carry it for trials at Herne Bay. After many disappointing drops using the Wellington, a Mosquito and a Lancaster, the technique and bomb were perfected. It had to be dropped accurately at a given height and rotated backwards before release. After long training on dams in Scotland, Wing Commander Guy Gibson VC led 617 Squadron on the famous 'Dam Busters' raid on 16th May 1943 which successfully breached the Mohne and Eder dams, made history and shortened the war.

Wellington development continued until 1945 when production ceased, using a variety of engines and to many specifications, the final being the Mk XVIII. The most common marks included the Mk II with

Sir Barnes Wallis, in the Brooklands clubhouse office. (Brooklands Museum)

A Vickers Warwick Air-Sea Rescue I variant, equipped with a lifeboat underneath. Note the similarity with a Wellington. (MAP)

Rolls-Royce Merlins, Mk III with Bristol Hercules, and Mk IV with Pratt and Whitney Twin Wasps. The Mk X, with the strengthened fuselage and Bristol Hercules VI or XVI of 1,675 hp giving greatly increased load and performance, was the most numerous of all the marks produced. The Mk V and Mk VI were the high altitude bombers with pressurised cabins. Wellingtons were the mainstay of Bomber Command in the early years of the war and were used at home also by Coastal Command in an anti-submarine and anti-magnetic mine role. They were also used overseas in the Middle and Far East. The reliable Wimpy was highly respected by its crews, it had the ability to withstand heavy battle damage and get them home, a tribute to the design team of Rex Pierson and Barnes Wallis. Out of a total of 11,460 produced, more than any other bomber, 2,514 were made at Brooklands.

The Warwick did not enter production until 1941, when a contract was placed for 250, delivery to commence in November. The first aircraft were produced using Pratt and Whitney Twin Wasps and later using those of Bristol Centaurus, but by the time the Warwick entered service it was too late for the heavy bomber role. The four-engined Lancasters, Halifaxes and Stirlings were already operating and the Warwick was switched to air-sea rescue and transport duties. A high altitude version was called for, and a four-engined aircraft with a pressurised cabin, the Windsor, was produced and proved very promising but with the ending of the war in the Pacific, production ceased after three had been built.

By 1942 space at Brooklands had become limited and a hangar for building experimental types was erected between Weybridge and Wisley, known as Foxwarren. Vickers' last fighter design to reach prototype flying was built here, the Type 432, a twin-engine (Rolls-Royce Merlin 61) high altitude fighter, very similar to the Mosquito in looks but of stressed skin construction and a modified geodetic wing. It was first flown in December 1942 by Tommy Lucke, a Vickers test pilot, but further work was cancelled in 1943.

Vickers also developed a large grass field three miles south-west of Brooklands at Wisley, which was put into service to handle the flight testing of aeroplanes built at Brooklands and their subsequent storage.

They were now turning their thoughts to civil aircraft for the post-war market, and used the expertise gained from the Wellington development to produce by 1944 a twin-engined aircraft. Named the Viking, it had a stressed skin fuselage and a fabric-covered Wellington-type wing with two Bristol Hercules 10M engines. The chief designer was now George Edwards (later Sir George), Rex Pierson having been made chief engineer, and the first prototype was flown by 'Mutt' Summers from Wisley on 22nd June 1945, the first post-war airliner to fly. It was soon in service with British European Airways and other airlines, and it also flew with the RAF as the Valetta and the larger Varsity.

The next to be flown by Summers, in 1948, was the prototype of the revolutionary Viscount, the first turbo-prop airliner. Vickers had now purchased Brooklands, laid a hard runway and expanded their production buildings, but the political situation was such that a nuclear bomb deterrent was felt to be necessary and the 'V' bomber force was born. The Valiant was produced, the first of a trio of jet 'V' bombers, in 1951 at Brooklands and test flown from Wisley by Summers.

The Vanguard was the next aircraft produced at Brooklands, a larger turbo-prop aircraft and replacement for the Viscount, but came too late as the pure jet aircraft were now taking over. The ill-fated TSR 2, a joint venture between Vickers and English Electric in 1957 was built at Brooklands and test flown at Boscombe Down in 1964. The most sophisticated strike and reconnaissance bomber, capable of Mach 2, it was axed in 1965 on government policy.

Vickers was now part of the British Aircraft Corporation, formed in

1960, and to offset the disappointment of the TSR 2 cancellation was producing a small quantity of BAC 111 jet airliners, as well as their own worldbeating VC 10 and later the Super VC 10. New buildings were erected, one ('The Cathedral') over the old sewage farm. However, the VC 10s were to be the last aircraft produced wholly by Vickers. In 1970 the last Super VC 10 left Brooklands for Wisley and the airfield closed for flying. Vickers now concentrated on making sections of Concorde – the nose, flight deck and fuselage. In 1977 Vickers became part of British Aerospace with Brooklands as its headquarters, continuing manufacturing aircraft components there until 1987 when the site closed, marking the demise of the first aerodrome in England.

Redevelopment began soon afterwards with the building of an industrial estate and busy roads now cross the runway. But the 'Spirit of Brooklands' is not forgotten, kept alive by the imaginative Brooklands Museum housed in some of the original buildings and part of the motor racing track in the north-east corner of the site. The old Brooklands clubhouse remains, the rooms set out in the style of its golden era along with motoring memorabilia of that period. In an adjacent hangar are many interesting aircraft, one a Brooklands-built Wellington, R for Robert, rescued from the depths of Loch Ness where it crashed during the war and now being completely restored.

9

OTHER AIRFIELDS AND SITES

Horne

In 1940, with the Battle of Britain in progress, it was felt that emergency landing grounds might be required in the south-east in case the main RAF aerodromes were put out of action. None were built at the time but when the RAF went on the offensive in 1941, the location of suitable sites for Advanced Landing Grounds, close to the south coast where aircraft could land, refuel and rearm, were investigated. A survey was carried out in 1942 with a view to assisting in Project Hadrian, a proposed landing in the Pas de Calais area. The projected airfields would be basic in construction, just two grass intersecting runways with perimeter tracks strengthened with metal tracking, with two or four Blister hangars and tented accommodation for personnel.

Following the disastrous raid on Dieppe in 1942, Project Hadrian was postponed but the survey for suitable sites went ahead in preparation for the full scale invasion of Europe. The search was made from Weston Super Mare across southern England to Frinton in Essex and 72 possibles were put forward for consideration. Finally this was reduced to 23, no doubt due to the fact that many were rich farmland and so objected to by the War Agricultural Committee. Two on the final list were situated in Surrey, both near to permanent RAF aerodromes, which would be important for servicing and repair work. The site at Dunsfold was selected for the building of a permanent aerodrome, leaving only the site at Horne for conversion to an ALG, with Redhill as its parent station and Kenley for repairs.

On 30th December 1943, No 4749 Flight of 5004 Works Squadron arrived at Redhill to commence work on a few acres of farmland straddling Bones Lane to the south of the village of Horne. The personnel were billeted along Nutfield Ridge, picked up each morning by coach at 6.30 am, taken to Redhill for breakfast then on to the site where the day was spent grubbing out trees and hedges. A small stream also had to be diverted before the ground was finally rolled to form two intersecting runways, finally covered with three-inch square mesh track. Perimeter tracks were laid, four Blister hangars were built, 24,000 gallons of fuel were stored and numerous Nissen huts housed the operations room etc. The site was ready on the 24th March but some work carried on until May.

On 28th March 1944, Flying Officer J. Williams arrived to take charge of No 142 Airfield. At the time it consisted of Typhoons and Mosquitos but it was felt these were not suited to ALG operation and it was decided instead that three lodger squadrons of No 11 Group, ADGB would occupy Horne, under the direction of No 142 Airfield staff.

On 30th April three Spitfire squadrons arrived – 130 Squadron with 21 Vcs and an Airspeed Oxford, 303 (Polish) Squadron with 21 Vbs, and 402 (Canadian) Squadron with 16 Vbs and four Vcs. Over 60 aircraft had to be dispersed around the airfield and the pilots and personnel housed in tents with primitive washing facilities. Flying operations were controlled by a caravan sited at the intersection of the runways. On 1st May Wing Commander Chalmers-Watson AFC arrived as permanent camp commandant and J. Checketts DSO, DFC, a New Zealander, as Wing Commander (Flying).

The defence of the airfield was carried out by a detachment of twelve members of RAF Regiment No 2877 with Hispano cannon and Browning machine guns dispersed around the field.

It was an extremely cold May, sleeping accommodation was spartan and ice formed on the water buckets outside for washing. However, on 2nd May the airfield was operational and 142 Wing took part in its first sortie, a Ramrod escorting Douglas Bostons to bomb Tournai at 12,000 feet. Flying to Manston, they had their long-range tanks topped up before meeting up with the Bostons.

Although Air Defence of Great Britain squadrons, they would be

RAF Horne (ALG) in May 1944. The tented accommodation of the ground crew of 402 Squadron is on the right, with the large mess tent in the centre. 303 Squadron's Spitfires can be seen on the left. (B. Buss)

engaged on offensive operations, and not all were Ramrods. On 2nd June, twelve Spitfires of 303 Squadron took off before daybreak, taxiing in the dark with only the lights of the aircraft in front for guidance, to rendezvous with Beaufighters over Dungeness. The Beaufighters were carrying torpedoes and everyone arrived in a gaggle of milling aircraft in the semi-darkness, eventually sorting themselves out to fly at 300 to 500 feet from Dieppe to Barfleur in search of convoys making a run for it in the dark. With no luck they returned to Horne at dawn and the crews went to bed fully dressed to defeat the cold.

The Spitfire Vbs and Vcs were often used to their best advantage low down in fighter sweeps. Often at the conclusion of a Ramrod perhaps a full wing of 36 aircraft in formation would fly very low, hugging the ground looking for targets of opportunity. On one such sweep over northern France, Flying Officer W. Hervey of 402 Squadron in a formation of about 40 aircraft line abreast, was searching for targets when he spotted a locomotive. Managing a short burst at the target he was himself attacked by fire from a flak tower. With very little room to manoeuvre for fear of collision, he let fly at the tower with the two cannon and four machine guns but high ground was greeting him fast.

With full power he climbed quickly through the low cloud and into the sunshine. Fearing for his comrades he called on the R/T but was promptly told to shut up! All aircraft returned safely.

On 21st May the three squadrons took part in a large sweep of about 500 aircraft. It proved to be a fateful day for the wing, who were attacking communication systems, trains and road vehicles north of the river Loire. Pilot Officer P. McCarthy of 130 Squadron recalls flying to Manston for fuel, crossing the Channel at 10,000 feet and then coming down almost to ground level. His section were following a road when he fired at a lorry containing troops.

Suddenly there was a loud bang, his aircraft shook and he realised his left arm was hit. His wingman alongside was also hit and was last seen trying to open the cockpit canopy. At treetop height, McCarthy turned to face what he thought were enemy fighters on his tail but to his amazement he found he was flying over an AA battery. Firing at them as he went over, he successfully climbed into cloud. After a while he broke through the cloud, only to find four aircraft in front in loose formation. Assuming they were bandits he had closed up for the attack when he realised they were his own squadron! Joining them, he flew back to Horne and was taken to Smallfields hospital.

Meanwhile, Pilot Officer Barny Barnard of 402 Squadron, whilst strafing a Ju 88 on the ground at Achiet aerodrome, was hit in the foot and sustained damage to his aircraft's air pressure system. Having no flaps and brakes he elected to land at Hawkinge and on landing found a bullet had penetrated his boot. He was taken to hospital. 303 Squadron also had their share of losses when a section led by Squadron Leader Koc ran into heavy gunfire. Flight Sergeant Wiktor Kempka was hit immediately and crashed in a field, while Flight Lieutenant S. Brzeski was hit and managed to climb before baling out. Both pilots survived and became POWs. Flight Sergeant Bezwluklo's aircraft was damaged but he managed to get the Spitfire back to another airfield in southern England. Flight Sergeant Bob Badkin, 'Mac' McCarthy's wingman, was hit at the same time by the flak and managed to belly land his Spitfire in a field not far from the AA battery. Quickly jumping from his aircraft, he tried to destroy it by using the incendiary device provided, but try as he may it would not ignite. Suddenly a machine gun opened up and a small detachment of soldiers from the AA battery appeared. He was taken away to the nearby town of St Pol and eventually to Stalag Luft 7, where he and Kempka both spent the war.

Life back at Horne was primitive with no recreational facilities so whenever possible personnel would visit the local school at Court Lees

A Spitfire squadron take-off at Horne, June 1944. (B. Buss)

for a hot shower, or the swimming baths at the Wagon at Horley. For light relief, the Blue Anchor (now the Parson's Pig) and the Jolly Farmers public houses were favourite watering holes.

As D-Day approached the squadrons' operations changed and they were required to mount dawn and dusk patrols along the south coast in flights of four to eight aircraft. Taking off in the dark and landing in the dark, they navigated by vectors supplied by Tangmere or Manston control. On the day before D-Day the aircraft were painted with black and white recognition stripes, leave was cancelled, plans collected from Tangmere and crews briefed. On 6th June, 124 Wing put up its first patrol at 3.42 am, over the beaches at low level. These continued throughout the day. Then for the next few days they continued their dawn and dusk patrols protecting the troops and convoys of equipment below. They flew low enough to be waved at, sometimes over British troops to the east or the Americans to the west. When the beach-heads were secured the squadrons went in search of enemy targets, mainly lorries and equipment.

Back home the crews worked feverishly out in the open to maintain the aircraft and keep them flying, those badly damaged being flown or transported to Kenley where workshop facilities existed. Most damage was from the heavy flak encountered, mainly at low level, but as the

179

A prototype V1 recovered and restored by Lashenden Air Warfare Museum. (Author)

invasion progressed enemy aircraft were encountered. Wing Commander Checketts damaged a Me 109 on 8th June, and on the 10th the wing claimed its first plane, destroyed by Pilot Officer R. Meadows of 130 Squadron.

Keen to confirm his victory he went back to photograph the wreckage but was unfortunately hit by our own fire. He landed safely at an ALG in France and returned by boat.

That Saturday was a bad day for 130 Squadron. One aircraft was seen to dive into the ground after jettisoning a slipper tank, and another two tragically collided in cloud. Squadron Leader W. Ireson, their commanding officer, was hit by flak from two American warships after breaking cloud near to the Isle of Wight. The aircraft was about to catch fire when he baled out near to a small vessel and was picked up and taken to France, where he boarded a ship back to England. With his uniform a bright yellow from the marker dye, he was eyed strangely in the train back to Redhill, but he made it safely back to Horne where a bottle of scotch welcomed his return.

The patrols continued until 15th June when the first V1s flew across the airfield. Interception patrols were mounted but the bombs were too fast for the Spitfire Vbs and Vcs. The shrapnel from the AA guns also made life uncomfortable as it rained down on the tents below. As the

OTHER AIRFIELDS AND SITES

risk increased to airfield personnel and aircraft, it was decided on 18th June to move out the next day, but not before the RAF Regiment bagged a V1 with machine gun fire. On the 19th, No 142 Airfield moved out to Tangmere and by the 24th the RAF Regiment and the rest of the personnel had also gone, leaving the airfield empty. As the V1 threat increased, the counter measure of a balloon barrage from Cobham, Kent now extended to Redhill, which became No 24 Balloon Centre. On 2nd July balloons were flown from Redhill and Horne and all aircraft landings at these airfields were stopped. This lasted until 31st August when the balloons were finally moved out.

Horne airfield's operational life lasted only seven weeks in May and June 1944 but during that time it provided the vital air cover needed over the beach-heads and an escort for the many Allied bomber raids. The estimated total of operational sorties flown was around 3,000. By August the remaining fuel had been removed and later the army track was taken away and the land reverted to its original use.

Driving down Bones Lane today, open fencing is seen where the runways crossed the road. In September 1994 a plaque was erected alongside the lane where the southernmost track once crossed it. The plaque displays the crests of the three squadrons and an airfield site plan.

Cobham and Fairchilds Farm

In 1943 with the formation of the 2nd Tactical Air Force, seven Army Observation Post squadrons were absorbed – 653, 658, 659 and 662 to No 83 Group and 652, 660 and 611 to No 84 Group. Equipped with Auster light aircraft, their role was to follow closely the invasion force and act as artillery spotters and reconnaissance, moving up with the army and operating from any suitable grass field or road on or near the front line and at very low level. Often subjected to heavy small arms and ground fire as well as fighters, their losses at times were heavy.

The Auster built in the UK was based on the American Taylorcraft Model C, a high-wing monoplane having two or three seats. In 1943 the AOP squadrons were equipped with the Auster Mk III with a Gipsy Major engine but these were later replaced with the Mk IV or V with the Lycoming 0-290 engine. In the hands of a skilled pilot, very short take-offs and landings could be made from small fields. In early 1944 the squadrons moved to their final marshalling areas close to the south coast to prepare for an instant call to France. The marshalling areas were unprepared sites, farmers' fields, playing fields, the grounds of country houses etc, and two sites were chosen in Surrey.

The old polo ground at Stoke D'Abernon, two miles to the east of Cobham was first used for a short while by 110 (AC) Squadron, RCAF, whose Lysanders based at Odiham used it as an ALG on 6th September 1940, serving the 1st Canadian Army HQ nearby at Headly Court. Later it became the home of 652 (AOP) Squadron with its Auster Mk IIIs, which arrived from Denham on 29th April 1944. The squadron had been training with army units similar to those it would be serving with in France, carrying out practice artillery shoots, reconnaissance and other tasks. They spent the next three weeks making preparations for the final move, checking and waterproofing their aircraft and equipment. On 27th May, the air party moved to Old Sarum but on 6th June, D-Day, at 12.30 pm the first ground party arrived on the French beaches and proceeded to the secured landing strip at Beny sur Mer. There was considerable enemy activity and they also had to fight with the army for possession, but it was secured and the vehicles moved in the next day. By the 8th, four Austers had landed and started operations, with seven shoots during the day. They lost their first aircraft and crew on 9th June when five Fw 190s attacked one Auster. Another on the 13th was brought down by small arms fire. On the 23rd, two more Austers were shot down by Me 109s.

An Auster Mk III with invasion stripes as used by the AOP squadrons of the 2nd TAF at Cobham and Fairchilds Farm. (Museum of Army Flying, Middle Wallop)

182

The Focke-Wulf FW 190, probably the most successful Luftwaffe fighter used during the war. (MAP)

The other marshalling area was at Fairchilds Farm, situated just inside the Surrey border, one mile to the west of Biggin Hill aerodrome. On 7th February 1944, 661 (AOP) Squadron's advance party moved in and on the 13th, twelve Auster Mk IIIs and a Tiger Moth flew in from Middle Wallop and were soon engaged in working up exercises for the coming invasion.

In the early days of the war the Austers were very basic in their equipment, having few instruments, and army pilots would fly by map and compass and the seat of their pants. One old pilot remembers that it was 1942 before artificial horizons were fitted. Quick and accurate map reading was essential when on reconnaissance or artillery spotting, together with the ability to make accurate fixes and targets on new ground when the army was advancing. One eye-sharpening exercise given in training was spotting small objects, an orange or bottle perhaps, in a field at a given map reference. However, it was also soon recognised that squadrons might have to move across the Channel quickly in bad weather or at night and an intensive programme of night flying was instituted at nearby Biggin Hill. The aircraft were fitted out for instrument and night flying and also embarked on a training exercise codenamed Pongo. Pilots had to be able to fly 50 miles across water on instruments, using direction finding equipment – for training purposes the Bristol Channel represented the English Channel and Wales represented France.

Training continued until 25th July when 661 Squadron moved out to France to commence operations. On one occasion on patrol over Boulogne, an Auster was hit by ground fire, damaging the throttle and wounding the pilot. The NCO observer in the rear seat operating the radio, leaned over and in co-operation with the wounded pilot managed to land the aircraft successfully.

As the AOP squadrons moved up with the armies through Europe, their fragile unarmed aircraft out in the front showing the way, the marshalling areas in Surrey reverted to their former use.

Kingston

Although not an airfield, mention must be made of one of the largest aircraft production sites in the country, with associations with Brooklands and later Dunsfold.

Aircraft production has been associated with Kingston since the First World War, when Mr Thomas (later Sir Thomas) Sopwith established his Sopwith Aviation Company in Canbury Park Road, transporting the aircraft to Brooklands for test flying. The testing was carried out by a young Australian, Harry Hawker, who had joined the company when they were producing at Brooklands, in 1912. Production at the Canbury Park Road site was prolific and by 1917 was such that new enlarged premises were acquired in Richmond Road about a mile away. After the war, in 1920 the company went into liquidation and a new company was formed, H. G. Hawker Engineering Company Ltd. In 1921 Harry Hawker was tragically killed in a flying accident but the company continued, and in 1923 young designer Sydney (later Sir Sydney) Camm joined. By 1925 he had become their chief designer.

In 1928 the market for aircraft was still depressed and the Richmond Road site was let out to the Leyland Motor Company, aircraft production and offices being restricted to the Canbury Park Road site. Here Sydney Camm produced many fine aircraft – the Horsley, the Hart family leading to the Fury, and by 1935 the Hurricane. When war commenced the Hawker factory at Canbury Park Road was producing Hurricanes and continued to do so until 1944, when new aircraft came

The principal Hawker works in Richmond Road, Kingston on Thames. (Kingston Heritage Services)

along – the Typhoon, Tempest and Sea Fury. At the same time at the Richmond Road works Leyland had been producing the Cromwell and Churchill tanks.

In 1948 Hawkers needed more space and moved back to the Richmond Road site, ceasing aircraft production at the Canbury Park Road site which it leased to other businesses. A new generation of jet fighters was produced at Richmond Road and transported to Dunsfold for erection and flying, including the Sea Hawk, the beautiful and successful Hunter, and the fabulous 'jump jet', the Harrier.

Over its history the original Hawker company has been absorbed by many companies and had many name changes, finally becoming part of British Aerospace. The large Richmond Road site functioned until 1992 when it closed, signalling the end of Kingston's long association with aircraft production. Both sites have now been redeveloped, with only the canteen at the Richmond Road site remaining. This was refurbished as a leisure centre for the people of Kingston and perpetuates a proud memory as 'The Hawker Centre'.

Wisley

In 1943 Vickers Aircraft Ltd at Weybridge began using a large grass airfield about three miles south of Brooklands as an extension to their premises. It was discovered by accident when 'Mutt' Summers some years previously had been flight testing a Wellesley and a problem developed on take off. The field presented itself and he made a successful landing. Later, bearing this in mind, Vickers surveyed the field and found that a runway of about 2,300 yards could be used. Aircraft from the production line, often in basic form, would be flown or transported from Brooklands to Wisley for erecting or fitting out. They were then flight tested and stored ready for collection by ATA pilots, often women, their diminutive stature dwarfed by the size of the bombers they flew out.

After the war the longer runway facilities were used more and more as the size of the aircraft being designed grew and by 1952 a hard runway was laid. Buildings in which to erect and maintain aircraft were put up and Wisley became the main flight testing centre for Weybridge-built aircraft, including the Viking, Viscount, Valiant, Vanguard, BAC 111 and the VC 10. However, situated near to the expanding Heathrow it eventually became no longer practical to

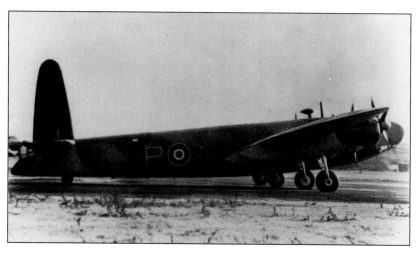

A Vickers Windsor, DW 412 second prototype, four-engine high altitude bomber, first flown from Wisley 15th February 1944 by 'Mutt' Summers. (MAP)

186

operate as a flight testing airfield and so in 1973 the British Aircraft Corporation closed Wisley. All the buildings have gone but the runway and VOR beacon still remain.

10
CIVILIANS
AT WAR

For centuries the people of the British Isles had been safe in their homes from the direct effects of war, surrounded by the sea and with a mighty Navy for protection. Yet with the birth of the flying machine all that had changed within just a few years. The horrors of war could now be brought to their doorstep by the bomber, as was proved by the airship and then the aeroplane in the First World War. Britain was no longer unassailable and the Navy alone could not protect her from this new and terrible form of warfare.

In the early 1930s it was realised that victory in future wars would depend on air power and in 1932 the Prime Minister at the time, Mr Stanley Baldwin foretold in a pessimistic and frightening speech that 'the bomber will always get through'. The outcome of a war would depend on who struck first and knocked out the opposing enemy. Though this view was not held by everyone, it was a fair assumption that some bombers would get through some of the time, and that strengthening of the armed forces alone would not be sufficient in future wars. Protection for the civilian population, cities, factories and the national infrastructure must also be considered if the nation was to survive.

By 1936 the clouds of war were gathering over Europe and Britain's rearmament programme was gaining pace. The Air Force had been reorganised and the accent was on defence against air attack. Already the effect of bombing had been seen in Abyssinia and Spain and in 1937 the Air Raid Precautions Act was passed to implement the necessary measures against air attack and to make the general public aware of what might happen in the event of war.

After the Munich crisis in 1938 a conflict in Europe began to seem

An ARP demonstration at Lorne Gardens, Shirley, 1939, showing decontamination procedure after a gas attack. (Croydon Local Studies Library)

inevitable and a few months later, in early 1939, the country was put on a war footing. Sir John Anderson was in charge of the civil defence of the country. The National Service Committee was formed under the Air Raid Precautions Act and the first ARP volunteers, air raid wardens, auxiliary firemen, first aiders, rescue and demolition workers were recruited. The fear of gas being used haunted everyone and in consequence gas masks were issued, some 38 million nationwide.

Protection from bombing for civilians was considered and each householder was provided with a shelter constructed from corrugated steel sheet, to be sunk into the ground and covered with earth. It was known as the Anderson shelter. Later in the war, for people without a garden, an indoor shelter similar to a reinforced table (and doubling as such) was provided and named after Herbert Morrison, now in charge of civil defence.

In streets and parks, and at the 1939 Empire Air Displays, lectures and demonstrations were given to the public on how to deal with incendiary bombs and effect decontamination after a gas attack. In April, conscription into the armed forces began for young men aged 18 years of age.

As tension mounted in Europe, trenches and public air raid shelters were dug in parks and open spaces. Important buildings were sandbagged and windows were criss-crossed with sticky tape to minimise danger from flying glass. Large storage tanks for emergency water supplies for fire fighting were situated at strategic points, and air raid sirens were erected near to police boxes and tested regularly.

For ARP services the County of Surrey was divided into two areas, one defined by the Metropolitan Police and known as the Eastern Emergency Area, the other by the Surrey Constabulary, known as the Western Emergency Area. In September 1939 each area appointed a War Emergency Committee and a Controller. The Eastern Area later became Group 9 of the London Civil Defence Area and had its control room in County Hall, Kingston. The Western Area was grouped with Reading Group 6, having its control room at Dorking, but in 1941 was amalgamated into the invasion area with Kent and Sussex and linked to the main regional control in Tunbridge Wells. Each borough or area had a control room linked to the regional control. Each street or area had its air raid wardens' post. The wardens supervised air raid precautions in their area, enforced the blackout and reported incidents back to the control room who would organise any emergency services required.

Plans for evacuating children from London and other cities and areas close to military targets were in place. It was thought that air attacks would come from over the North Sea, therefore the flight paths of enemy bombers would be over Kent and Essex and the evacuation of Surrey children from the metropolitan areas was to be to the more rural 'safe' areas to the south and west of the county and to the south coast. No one foresaw the possibility of the fall of France, with the consequence of enemy airfields spread right along the Channel coast and Surrey in as much of a straight line to London as Kent or Essex.

On 24th August the General Powers Act was passed, giving wide powers to local authorities to enforce any measures they thought necessary for national safety. Reservists were called up and the ARP brought to a state of readiness. Control rooms were manned with officers, telephonists and other staff.

Britain and France had issued an ultimatum to Germany over the occupation of Poland and the nation waited. On 1st September, German troops invaded Poland and war seemed inevitable. Schools closed and the evacuation of children from London and the priority areas of Surrey around Barnes, Merton, Morden, Mitcham and Wimbledon began. Over 6,000 persons were moved to the 'safe' reception areas in the south and west of the county and on the south coast before war started. Blackout regulations were now enforced.

The ultimatum to Germany over the occupation of Poland expired on 3rd September 1939 at 11 am and when no message was received from Hitler, the Prime Minister, Mr Neville Chamberlain broadcast to the nation at 11.15 am 'that a state of war existed'. When the sirens sounded 15 minutes later for the first time there was no panic, just a slight bewilderment with citizens not knowing what to do and what to expect. This time it was a false alarm and the expected air attacks did not immediately materialise.

Members of voluntary organisations reported to their control centres for instructions and everyone was glued to the wireless set for more information; the news bulletins became the focal point of each day. What would war bring? Stories and pictures of what had happened to other European cities were fresh in people's minds. The threat of air raids was thought to be imminent and every night at dusk, preparation began for a vigil in the Anderson shelter. Warm clothes, balaclava helmets, a thermos flask and a torch were essentials. Getting used to the blackout was another problem and the cry, 'Put that light out' was often heard. All road vehicles travelled at night with subdued headlights and buses and trains had very dim blue interior lights and blacked out windows. As an added hardship, petrol rationing was in force.

As the days and weeks progressed with no air raids, some normality returned. Cinemas and theatres reopened. Schools which had been closed now opened on a limited scale, pupils attending the one nearest their home. There was activity at sea and some tragic losses occurred with the sinking of the *Athenia* and HMS *Royal Oak*, but the battlefields remained quiet and the RAF were delivering only leaflets over Germany. Due to the relative inactivity some people remarked, 'It will be over by Christmas.' It wasn't, but many returned to sleeping indoors and became blase about carrying gas masks. Hundreds of evacuees returned home.

In the new year of 1940 the war began to bite in the home. Food rationing had begun in November with bacon and butter and now sugar, ham, meat and cheese were added to the list. That winter was very cold and fuel was scarce. The wireless, the focal point of many homes, continued to issue official communiques. The Radio Doctor gave advice on health and the Ministry of Food gave tips and recipes on how to make the most of the rations. Potatoes were in good supply and formed the basis of many meals.

Croydon men answer the call and join the Local Defence Volunteers in May 1940 (later the Home Guard). (Croydon Local Studies Library)

On 10th May 1940, early morning listeners to the BBC were stunned by the news that German bombers were attacking a range of targets in neutral Holland, Belgium and Luxembourg, as well as France. Paratroops were being used to gain vantage points such as aerodromes to allow troop transport planes to land. The British Expeditionary Force and French army fought valiantly but were soon cut off by the speed of the German advance to the Channel through Belgium and Holland. Their backs to the sea, our troops became concentrated in the Calais-Dunkirk area.

At home the threat of invasion was considered a very real danger and on 14th May, the Secretary for War, Mr Anthony Eden warned against paratroops landing and called for every able-bodied man between 17 and 65 to join the Local Defence Volunteers. The men of Surrey responded immediately, reporting to their local police station to sign on. They carried a motley collection of weapons, including shotguns, sporting guns and war trophies. Redhill and Reigate had 800 men volunteer in the first 24 hours and this was typical over the county. Nationally, in the first week over a quarter of a million men enrolled in what Winston Churchill called the Home Guard. Nicknamed 'Dad's Army', this volunteer band turned into a highly trained force, soon taking over at home many of the duties of the regular army.

On 26th May the urgent decision was made to bring home the BEF from France and Operation Dynamo swung into action. The epic evacuation of 338,226 British and Allied troops from the beaches of Dunkirk is known to everyone. For the people of Surrey, the first images of war emerged. Many of the evacuated troops were landed at Dover and Folkestone and placed on waiting trains. One after the other they steamed up the main Ashford-Redhill railway line, the engine of one train almost touching the guards van of the one in front.

Redhill became one of the main receiving stations for the battle-weary heroes, who were dirty and dishevelled. Many were wounded. The people of Redhill turned out to cheer them and do what they could, with the voluntary services serving each with a 'cuppa' and sandwiches. Some of the wounded were taken from the train and transported to local hospitals. Redhill aerodrome received many of the men for feeding and rekitting before moving on, and the station staff at Redhill worked furiously to replenish coal and water for the engines to send them on their way.

The county tensed itself for the threat of imminent invasion. Mr Churchill's inspiring message to the nation on 4th June – 'We shall defend our island, whatever the cost may be. We shall fight on the beaches, we shall fight on the landing grounds, we shall fight in the fields ...' – emphasised the gravity of the situation. Local defence measures were strengthened and road blocks set up. Open ground was protected against landing enemy aircraft and gliders by dumping old cars or driving poles into the ground. Road signs and street names were removed. Civilians had restricted access to some roads near to military installations, and identity cards had to be produced on demand. By July the Home Guard, now a strong and organised force, had taken over many of the army's duties. The people now waited.

Rationing bit harder. Cooking fats were rationed, butter and margarine only 6 oz a week, and Britain's panacea for all situations, tea, was only 2 oz a week. Everyone was urged to save in the National Savings scheme, contribute to the Spitfire fund, Dig for Victory, save waste paper and give up aluminium saucepans for salvage.

On 10th July 1940 the Luftwaffe intensified their operations to destroy the RAF prior to invasion, with raids on Channel shipping and coastal towns. Probing raids inland had begun as early as April, but on 24th July the first bombs fell on Surrey at Walton on Thames.

When the Channel operations failed, the raids moved inland on 12th

Women operate the telephones in the Message Room of the Civil Defence control centre in County Hall, Kingston on Thames. Note the gas mask at the ready. (Surrey Record Office)

August to airfields and aircraft production centres, with the accompanying threat to surrounding civilian areas. On 3rd August, Walton school was hit and on the 4th, Whitely village. On the 5th German bombers were in the Weybridge area, no doubt looking for the well camouflaged site of Brooklands, housing Vickers and Hawker aircraft production. The raids intensified during the month as they moved further inland.

The 15th was a warm sunny day and the evening was quiet, with a summer haze. Enemy activity had been heavy during the day, operating from their bases from Norway to France. This evening they were about to concentrate on the South East. At around 6.50 pm, 111 Squadron took off from Croydon on a yellow alert. People watched as they strolled, many coming home from work. Those walking near to the airport then heard the sound of engines and saw about 20 aircraft overhead. 'Ours', was the general opinion until objects were seen to fall from them, followed by loud explosions.

German aircraft were diving onto Croydon airport, machine gunning and bombing. At the same time they were being attacked by 111 Squadron who had been patrolling overhead, and in the ensuing panic,

The Bourjois cosmetic factory alongside Croydon airport, badly damaged in the raid of 15th August 1940. (LB of Sutton Heritage Service)

bombs were dropped wide of the target. Buses near to the Town Hall stopped and passengers took cover. Those in a bus in the Purley Way suddenly found they had grandstand seats of the frightening raid unfolding in front of them. No warning had been given and the attack was a complete surprise. The airport was surrounded by the large Waddon housing estate and many industries. Bombs overshooting the airport fell on the Redwing aircraft hangar, the NSF factory, the Bourjois cosmetic factory, Phillips, Mullard and many others. In the NSF factory the Board of Directors were meeting. They were killed instantly, along with many others, 35 in all.

Herbert Failes was then a young lad of 16 working for Rollasons, and also an ATC cadet. On the day of the raid he had been working at the head office, Woodcote House in Wallington and had to go to the airport office to help get the wages ready for the next day. He remembers:

'I cycled down about 5 pm and met Chris Rogers, who was a clerk the same as me. We were in an office at the back of the hangar. There were three of us in that evening, my friend Chris and a lady cleaner. I was standing up looking through the windows, the hangar doors were slightly open and I could see across the airfield and pilots running to their aircraft. I turned and said to Chris, "I think there must be a raid on." Within a few seconds, with no warning given, I heard the whistling of bombs being dropped, not realising what they were until the office turned upside down!

'We were on the first floor and I called, "Come on" to Chris and the lady, then saw a carpenter walking towards me who had been blown up through the floor. We managed to get out of the door but the staircase had been blown away, so I jumped to the floor below calling for the lady to follow but she refused. Chris and I ran across the hangar and dived under some aircraft on trestles for repair, then made for the doors. The hangar was full of smoke and dust and a strong smell of cordite but we kept running as they were still bombing, across the tarmac to the underground shelters.

'I was only 16 but was ordered to stand guard on a shelter where the firm's Home Guard had put some of their rifles and ammunition. I was allowed to go home at about 9 pm, but as my bicycle and jacket had been lost I had to borrow some money to get home to Selhurst on the trolley bus. Despite severe bruising I managed to get into work the next morning to hand out the wages.'

At the Bourjois soap factory a direct hit on the soap-making department killed three men. Bombs fell in Crowley Crescent, Coldharbour Way, Foss Avenue and Waddon Way with many fatalities. Rescue work continued for several days, when the total casualties were found to be 62 dead, 37 seriously injured and 137 with lighter injuries. Clearing up after the raid and finding shelter for the victims became an all too familiar scene in the coming months and years. On the same evening bombs fell in Reigate for the first time, injuring three cyclists.

On 16th August, a day of low cloud, planes were heard passing over Kingston in the afternoon and New Malden was heavily bombed, no doubt searching for the Hawker aircraft works in Canbury Park Road and in Richmond Road where Leyland were producing tanks. The railway station was badly hit and great damage was done to over 1,300 houses with many people killed. Wimbledon received an attack in the evening, bombs falling close to a cinema and housing, killing 14 people.

On the 18th, Kenley aerodrome was the target for a three-pronged attack which went wrong (see Kenley). The first civilian casualties of the raid resulted even before the aircraft reached their target. Along the route from the coast the Dorniers flew at rooftop height, machine gunning as they went. At Caterham one man was hit in the legs and a fleet of ambulances at Westaway fire station were put out of action.

Bombs began to fall before the raiders reached Kenley and three cottages were destroyed, with one lady being killed. During the raid a bungalow, Sunnycroft, was wrecked when a damaged Dornier fell on it but the occupants, although trapped inside, managed to escape. The Crest, a large house used as a machine gun post was demolished, trapping three soldiers inside. They were later dug out.

Towards the end of the month the enemy realised that the day offensive was not working, and they were suffering huge aircraft losses. They now turned to raiding by night. On the 24th, Kingston experienced its first air raid at midnight when eight bombs were dropped on Clarence Street, Eden Street and Avenue Road. Guildhall Control organised the emergency services quickly and, amazingly, there were no casualties. The raiders were still probing to find the local aircraft works and military targets, and between the end of August and the beginning of September there were many raids in the Weybridge area. Damage was done in the Chertsey area and to the south-west of Weybridge station. On the 24th, 13 high explosive and many incendiary bombs fell between Weylands sewage farm and Field Common, damaging Walton school and houses in Normanhurst Road. On the 29th, bombs fell in Whitely village.

On 4th September 1940, the Vickers works at Brooklands was attacked in daylight without warning. It was a warm sunny afternoon and men and women were enjoying their lunch break, sitting outside in the sun. Others were still in the canteen, or standing around the time clock in the machine shop waiting to clock-on for the beginning of the afternoon shift. A noise of aircraft was heard, thought to be Hurricanes from the Hawker site, but those sitting outside could see them and the bombs falling. There was no time to take cover. The first bombs fell behind the old grandstand and the others on the machine shop, causing a great number of fatalities. The canteen situated above the machine shop received the full effect of the blast and many more people there were killed or injured.

On the day of the raid a young Yorkshire girl was working in the tool room office on the ground floor. Today she lives in Weybridge, and vividly remembers the events that day:

'Lunch time came and everyone poured out onto St George's Hill, which was opposite the factory gates. It was a boiling hot day, and we all ate our sandwiches and laid out on the grass sunning ourselves and chatting. I only stayed for a short while as there was such a lot of work to get through. I had just got to the office, pulled a chair up to the desk, and wham! all hell broke loose.

'I was petrified. I couldn't see anything. All the machinery, desks, glass, cabinets, all came flying down. I tried to make it to the main doors which I knew were open. I was knocked over three times in the rush for the shelters and badly gashed my leg on broken glass. I got my hankie out and tied it around my leg.

'I did eventually get to the main doors. There were people going everywhere – absolute panic. I went straight across the road to the shelters which were underground. There was a first aid room there too, where lots of us had been coming on Sunday mornings learning first aid. The head one gave me a drink of water, then we went out and started loading up the injured into cars, lorries, ambulances. By this time my shoe was full of blood. We couldn't spare bandages. Somebody tied a scarf round my leg, emptied my shoe, put it back on, then shoved me in a lorry with six injured men. I was given a lemonade, a bottle of water, a piece of paper and a pencil. I had to try to get their names and works number. We went to Weybridge Hospital first. The police said, "Full up, try Walton." We did – the same answer. We went to Surbiton, Kingston, village after village. We ended up somewhere near London at a maternity home. They stitched my leg. Two of the men had died. We left them all there and went back to the factory for more. A lot of my friends were killed.'

Several other bombs fell, one on an air raid shelter. In total, 83 people died in the raid and 419 were injured, many seriously.

By 15th September 1940 the Battle had reached its climax – Hitler realised the RAF could not be beaten and the invasion of England was postponed. This gave no respite to the civilian population, however, as the raids switched to every night and the London Blitz began. This was to last well into the late spring of 1941.

Besides coping with this harrowing way of life, citizens were being urged to save money in National Savings, and to contribute to War Weapons Week or the Spitfire fund. Large indicator boards outside churches or town halls indicated the amount each borough had collected. Each £5,000 bought a Spitfire and £30,000 bought a tank. Shot-down German aircraft were exhibited and 3d or 6d was charged for admission, all contributing to the funds. Income tax rose and people were told to 'Dig for Victory' in their gardens or allotments, or take their holidays helping the farmers and the Land Army girls to bring in the harvest.

The Anderson shelter had without doubt proved its worth, saving many lives from bombs which had fallen only feet away. As the night raids became a regular way of life the shelters became a second home from dusk to dawn. Many had bunk beds, an electric light and wireless – which for a great deal of the time wasn't a lot of good, for as soon as a raid was imminent the BBC went off the air. However, condensation running down the walls, and in some cases flooding, could be a serious problem.

Evacuees had been brought back from the threatened south coast and relocated in safe areas. The whole of Mitcham was now included in the priority areas and by the end of 1940 a further 3,300 had been evacuated. The night raids continued throughout the winter but some semblance of normality was defiantly maintained. Cinemas and theatres remained open and trains and buses kept running. The post, the milk and the papers usually managed to be delivered as usual.

The enemy airfields in occupied France now stretched right down the Channel coast and the flight paths of the bombers took them directly over the county on their way to and from London and other cities. In September 1940 Kingston had a bad raid when bombs fell on Hodgsons Brewery and damaged most of the buildings in the town centre, but by far the worst-hit borough was Croydon. The raid on the aerodrome in August was followed later in the month when a lone raider scored a direct hit on the airfield, with another completely destroying the already damaged Bourjois factory.

The Germans were now using larger bombs, known as land mines. Dropped by parachute for maximum blast effect, the damage was fearful. Incendiary bombs were dropped by the thousands, weighing only one kilo each but sufficient to start a consuming fire if not dealt with quickly. Fire-watching became compulsory and sand and stirrup pumps were kept at hand to douse them before the fire took hold.

As the autumn wore on, many Surrey boroughs were hit by indiscriminate bombing, raiders jettisoning their bombs during attacks on London. On 10th October in the early evening, during a big raid, the canteen at County Hall was hit and three people killed and several injured. In November, Croydon Town Hall was hit, along with the Liberal Club, tragically killing 25 people. In the new year most areas were affected. In January 1941, Woking had its worst raid when bombs killed six people and in March land mines fell in Leatherhead, killing one person and injuring 27.

Aircraft continued to overfly the county en route for the cities of the Midlands and the North. On the night of 9th April 1941, a Heinkel 111, one of 300 making for Birmingham, was attacked by a Defiant night fighter of 264 Squadron and crash-landed at Lodge Bottom, Busbridge, near Godalming.

Bomb damage to the canteen of County Hall, Kingston on 10th October 1940, after a raid that killed three people. (Surrey Record Office)

There was now a quiet period until the night of 16th April when the Luftwaffe recommenced operations with an attack on Croydon. The sirens sounded at 9.30 pm and the whole borough was subjected to a savage attack by incendiary bombs and land mines until 4 am. Mr Berwick Sayers, chief librarian of the borough, says in *Croydon in the Second World War* that 'no one who survived the night is likely to forget it'. The fire brigade were called to 230 fires and also sent pumps to Beckenham and Clapham.

Out of the 60 major incidents the three worst involved land mines. One fell on the Queen's Road Homes for the old and sick. The building was badly damaged, 17 patients were killed and 31 injured, 11 of them seriously. The second mine fell on Limes Avenue in Waddon and caused great damage to Lodge Avenue and surrounding roads, and the third fell in Court Drive near to Waddon Ponds, wrecking four houses there and damaging all the houses in Ridge Way. Besides other widespread destruction, twelve delayed-action bombs fell spread over a wide area. This savage and indiscriminate attack accounted for 76 people killed and 156 injured.

On the night of 19th April the raiders returned and attacked West Croydon, Upper Norwood, Lower Addiscombe Road and Crohamhurst.

New Addington was also attacked. Two land mines also fell at Merstham with ten people killed and twelve injured plus great damage to buildings.

A lull followed until 10th May when the Luftwaffe mounted what proved to be the last big raid on London. With a full moon and excellent visibility, 550 raiding aircraft pounded London and the suburbs from around 10.50 pm to 5.50 am with incendiary and high explosive bombs. Early fires were started in Upper Norwood, Thornton Heath and Addiscombe but South Croydon received the heaviest attack. One bomb fell on an Anderson shelter, another on a varnish and polish store causing burning varnish to run down the road.

The most serious incident involved two bombs on the London Transport bus garage in the Brighton Road. The garage was full of buses with full tanks of petrol ready for the following morning. The building erupted in a fierce explosion of fire, trapping many of the men working inside. Some had jumped under the buses into the examination pits when the first bombs fell, others were blown into them by the blast. Many brave attempts were made to save these trapped men by the rescue squads. The Commandant of the stretcher depot, Mr H. Locke-Kendell, rescued three of them, returning four times, but his attempt to rescue two men in the pit under a blazing bus was in vain. For this act of heroism he was awarded a Royal Commendation. The garage was completely destroyed along with 65 buses. Fourteen people died in this ferocious night raid and 40 were severely injured. The raiders did not have it all their own way. The bomber's moon was also a great aid to the night fighters who claimed over 30 enemy aircraft destroyed.

When the all clear sounded, the work of tending to the dead and wounded began. Rescue and demolition squads continued for days searching the rubble, clearing the debris from the roads and making safe damaged buildings. They also had to repair essential services such as gas, water and electricity. The most important problem was the sheltering of people who had lost everything.

With the ending of the Blitz (Hitler had now turned his attention to the invasion of Russia) life began to return to some normality apart from sporadic raids. By now further restrictions meant that clothes were rationed, 24 coupons having to last seven months, with shoes taking seven coupons, a dress twelve coupons, and a coat 18 coupons. The 'utility' suit made its appearance for 18 coupons.

By the end of December 1941, Japan had attacked Pearl Harbour. America was now in the war and in January 1942 it was announced

A Heinkel He 111 of 11/KG55, shot down by a Defiant night fighter of 264 Squadron at Lodge Bottom, Busbridge, 9th April 1941. (H. Oltman, via A. Johnson)

that American forces would be sent to Britain. Tragic though it was for America, the British people now felt they were not alone, and that some positive outcome of the war might be in sight. Preparations for the invasion of Europe gained strength and many overseas forces were stationed in southern England. Surrey had been the home for Canadian soldiers since the beginning of the war and there were many Canadian squadrons stationed at the aerodromes. The locals got to know these friendly men from over the seas.

Sporadic 'hit and run' raids continued, often by fast fighter bombers such as the Me 109, Me 110 and the Fw 190, and sometimes by small formations of conventional bombers machine gunning and bombing. These attacks could strike anywhere at any time, often in conditions of low cloud when the aircraft could use cover for hide and seek. Rex Nicholls, who lived in Thornton Heath at the time, relates a typical attack:

'One day I was crossing the factory yard where I worked when the sound of overworked engines had everyone gazing skywards. Between a gap in the clouds we saw a Dornier 217. It opened fire with machine guns, reportedly hitting Church Street, Croydon, while a stick of bombs fell near my home a mile away ... One of its bombs struck the Power Samas factory about 300 yards from my home, killing seven workers. It was said the bomber was shot down at Caterham.'

The raids also struck at the rural 'safe' areas. In December 1942 a lone Dornier 217 in low cloud followed the branch railway line from Horsham to Guildford. It then machine gunned and bombed a small commuter train of two coaches packed with Christmas shoppers just outside Bramley station. Eye witnesses said the plane flew so low 'it could almost be touched'. Men rushed to help from the nearby coal yard and were soon joined by doctors, ARP wardens and a Canadian medical unit nearby. The village was deeply shocked at the savagery of the raid. Seven people were killed and the rest of the 47 passengers on the train injured.

In January 1944 the Luftwaffe mounted a surprising number of bomber attacks on London and the South East, the 'Mini-Blitz', which lasted for about three months. Fleets of about 100 aircraft took part in these raids with some towns in the county sustaining damage. However, the night fighter capability of the RAF was now highly efficient. Enemy losses were very high and the raids fizzled out by the summer.

On 6th June 1944 the Allies invaded Europe, but any joy or relief felt by the population at home was soon tinged with fear by the sudden

The damaged passenger train at Bramley which was shot at and bombed by a lone Dornier 217, in December 1942. (Middleton Press)

appearance of the flying bomb, the V1 or 'Doodlebug', one of Hitler's secret weapons. The 'Diver' first appeared on the night of 13th June, crossing the coast near Dymchurch and crashing at Swanscombe in Kent. First just a few, then coming by the hundreds, the first ones were seen over Surrey on the 16th and fell nearby on Worcester Park.

Launched from ramps in the Pas de Calais area, these pilotless aircraft with a one-ton warhead were powered by a pulse jet engine and flew at over 400 mph at a relatively low altitude towards London. When the engine stopped, the fiendish machine plunged or glided to earth. The noise of the V1 was unmistakable and never forgotten. The defences, unfamiliar with this new form of attack, at first allowed many of the bombs to get through but by August the destruction rate was over seventy per cent.

'Once the characteristics of the V1 had been noted,' recalls Rex Nicholls, 'they were, in a manner of speaking, easy to live with. They could always be heard approaching, for their engines were raucous. On most days, they could be seen and their progress watched. They would pass quite low overhead and could be studied quite dispassionately. Should the engine falter and stop the adrenalin immediately began to

Flying bomb damage at Hatch Road, Norbury on 22nd June 1944. (Croydon Local Studies Library)

flow! At work we took to the air raid shelter only when danger was imminent. At the height of the V1 campaign we would pencil five-bar gates on the walls to record each visit. The record was 32 in one nine and a half hour working day. One Saturday morning notched up 16 alerts.'

The attacks were continuous by day and night but the population could not live in shelters. Work and life had to continue. There was a great exodus from the areas affected, which included the Metropolitan area of Reigate, the rural area of Godstone and the urban areas of Caterham and Warlingham. By the end of 1944 the total number of children and others evacuated was over 77,000. Work continued, factories and work places having 'spotters' on the roofs or vantage points watching the paths of bombs and giving the signal to take cover when danger seemed imminent.

Mr G. Smith was a schoolboy in Purley during the V1 attacks and kept a diary:

'On the morning of Friday 16th June 1944 I saw my first flying bomb. It flashed across Purley straight as a die, making loud sinister noises and looking as if it knew what it was doing. It disappeared behind a hill still proceeding confidently. Everyone knew it was the long-

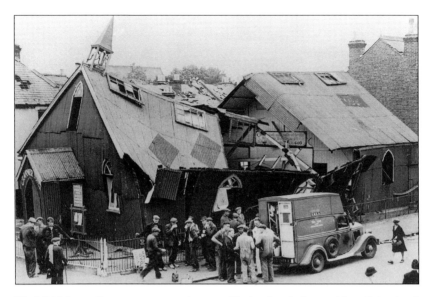

The YMCA van dispenses tea to workers outside the church damaged by a flying bomb in Cranmer Road, Croydon, 26th July 1944. (Croydon Local Studies Library)

expected secret weapon and I didn't feel happy about it at all.

'On Friday 23rd June matriculation exams started. At my school this exam was held in a large hall with windows on all sides and continued for several days. The flying bombs were coming over very frequently and we could not go to shelter – lest we cheat – when the school porter rang a bell we had to get underneath our desks. No extra time was allowed for these disruptions. This occurred three times during the English exam on 26th June, according to my diary.

'Exams ended on Wednesday 5th July at 4.10 pm (diary again). I was cycling home feeling rather relieved and was almost there when I noticed crossing the road ahead of me a large green flying bomb, gliding slowly at tree-top height and rocking gently from side to side. I immediately stopped to await events. There soon followed a very loud bang with bits flying everywhere and thick dust making it as dark as night. I remounted and pedalled rapidly towards the scene. The explosion was 600 yards ahead of me but I had been sheltered by the houses behind which the bomb had landed. It had fallen short of our house by a couple of hundred yards but my mother, who was out walking the dog, was really very close to it. She was unhurt though in some disarray – as was the dog. Nobody was hurt but my model aeroplane collection was flattened by the lounge ceiling falling upon it. The house was in a sorry state; just habitable but without windows. We were tough in those days and cycled to school taking cover if necessary. We were not allowed to be late, either.'

In the period 15th June to 16th August, by when the Allies had overrun most of the launch sites, 903 V1s had fallen in Surrey out of the total of 8,000 launched, 2,400 reaching the London area. Once again, Croydon took the brunt of the attack with 141 bombs falling in the borough, killing 211 people. The rest fell evenly over the county, even in the rural areas as far as Guildford to the west. Peter Stock lived in Godalming during the war and recalls:

'Quite a number landed indiscriminately, usually in open farmland and so little damage was done. We took little notice all the time the engine could be heard, but dived for cover when it stopped and an eerie silence fell, followed by the loud explosion. During the summer holidays, once I was old enough, I used to go with my sister to help on Mason's Farm. We were harvesting potatoes when we heard a bomb approaching. The farm foreman blew a whistle and we all dived into the nearest ditch as the engine cut out. The farm was on a hill and I lifted my head to peer through the hedge into the next field. I saw the

An Anderson shelter proving its worth saving lives in the flying bomb attack on Spring Park Road, Shirley on 26th July 1944. (Croydon Local Studies Library)

bomb a few yards away just skimming the crop and flying between two oak trees. It glided across the valley and exploded in woodland opposite.

'Another occasion was more serious. We had just finished breakfast when we heard a bomb coming, cut out, and then the sound of rushing air as it flew low overhead and crashed into trees adjoining Holloway Hill at the end of the road. Our ears were deafened and then the whole house shook and the windows flew open. Miraculously, none were broken. Two men were walking down Holloway Hill on their way to the station when the bomb exploded in a dell just a few feet away. They were both blown off the high path down into the road below with dozens of trees crashing down on top of them. When soldiers eventually got to the seriously injured men they were found to be riddled with thousands of splinters. They were in hospital for many months.'

By the first week in September the menace of the V1 attacks appeared to be almost over and people were returning to life indoors. The Allies were established in Europe, the end of the war seemed in sight and spirits rose. However, on 8th September 1944 two loud explosions were heard from incidents in Chiswick and Epping. The official explanation given at the time was that gas mains, damaged in the previous bombing, were exploding. Soon it was evident, however, that another new weapon was being used, not unexpected by the Government who had known of its existence from photo-reconnaissance. They had been reticent about informing and alarming the public, fearing the stress of yet another form of bombardment, when the war was nearly over, would prove intolerable.

There was no defence against the V2. Launched from sites in Holland, it reached a height of 50 miles, then on its descent attained supersonic speeds. Its one-ton warhead caused a great explosion, followed by an unfamiliar sonic boom. The rockets continued to fall. The first one in Surrey was at Coulsdon on 17th September, and another in Croydon, at Sunnybank in South Norwood, in October killed six people and caused great damage. The attitude of people towards the rocket attack was fatalistic. There was no warning of its coming or defence against its approach, and the attacks were random, falling over a wide area. The numbers were not great compared to the V1 attack and it was known that the Allies would soon overrun the launch sites. So people tried to continue as normal, though when incidents did occur casualties could be high.

The V2 attacks continued until March 1945, when all the launch sites

The first V2 rocket fell in the Croydon area on 20th October 1944, causing great damage at Sunnybank, South Norwood. (Croydon Local Studies Library)

had been captured – but not before 21 rockets had fallen in the county. Now with the end of the V1 and V2 menace, people felt the end of the war was in sight. There was some relaxation in rationing and the blackout regulations were eased. The Home Guard was disbanded.

By 4th May 1945, when the German forces surrendered, the country had endured six years of a people's war, one of the most savage in history, and had paid a heavy price for the victory. More than 60,000 civilians had been killed, 2,300 of them in the County of Surrey with thousands more injured or hurt. Everyone looked forward to the future and peace, but bomb-damaged homes and buildings, grim reminders of the past conflict, would remain in the cities and towns for many years to come.

Appendix

THE SQUADRONS AND UNITS THAT WERE BASED AT THE
SURREY AIRFIELDS DURING THE SECOND WORLD WAR

DUNSFOLD – 98 *(VO: Mitchell: Aug 43–Oct 44)*, 180 *(EV: Mitchell: Aug 43–Oct 44)*, 231 *(Mustang: Jul 43)*, 320 RDNAS *(TD: Mitchell: Feb 44–Oct 44)*, 400 RCAF *(SP: Mustang, Mosquito: Dec 42, Feb 43–Jul 43, Dec 43–Feb 44)*, 414 RCAF *(RU: Mustang: Dec 42–Apr 43, Jun 43–Jul 43)*, 430 RCAF *(Tomahawk, Mustang: Jan 43–Jul 43)*, 667 *(Oxford: Dec 45–Feb 46)*, 83 GSU *(7S: Typhoon, Tempest, Spitfire: Jan 45–Aug 45)*, 83 GDC *(Aug 45–Oct 45)*, 83 GSU Comm. Flight *(Anson: Mar 45–Aug 45)*.

REDHILL – 1 *(JX: Hurricane: May 41–Jun 41, Jun 41–Jul 41)*, 15 AC *(UC: Lysander: Jun 40)*, 50 AC *(Jun 40–Sep 40)*, 66 *(LZ: Spitfire: Aug 43)*, 131 *(NX: Spitfire: Aug 43)*, 166 *(Feb 45)*, 219 *(FK: Blenheim, Beaufighter: Oct 40–Dec 40)*, 258 *(ZT: Hurricane: Jun 40)*, 287 AC *(KZ: Feb 45)*, 303 *(RF: Spitfire: Aug 42)*, 310 *(NN: Spitfire: Aug 42)*, 312 *(DU: Spitfire: Aug 42)*, 350 *(MN: Spitfire: Jun 42–Aug 42)*, 401 *(YO: Spitfire: Jul 43–Aug 43)*, 402 *(AE: Spitfire: May 42–Aug 42)*, 411 *(DB: Spitfire: Apr 43–Aug 43)*, 412 *(VZ: Spitfire: Jul 43–Aug 43)*, 416 *(DN: Spitfire: Nov 42–Feb 43)*, 421 *(AV: Spitfire: May 43)*, 452 *(UD: Spitfire: Oct 41–Jan 42)*, 457 *(BP: Spitfire: Mar 42–May 42)*, 485 *(OU: Spitfire: Jul 41–Oct 41)*, 504 *(TM: Spitfire: Aug 43–Sep 43)*, 600 *(BQ: Blenheim, Beaufighter: Sep 40)*, 602 *(LO: Spitfire: Jan 42–Feb 42, May 42–Jul 42)*, 611 *(FY: Spitfire: Jul 42–Sep 42)*, 15 EFTS *(Hart, Magister: Sep 39–Jun 40)*, Polish Grading School *(Magister, Battle: Mar 40–Jun 40)*, 83 Gp. Comm. Sq. *(Hudson, Oxford, Anson: Nov 43–Apr 44)*, 84 Gp. Comm. Sq. *(Hudson, Oxford, Anson: Apr 44–May 44)*, 128 Airfield *(Mustang: Nov 43–Feb 44)*, 1210 Transport Flt. *(Anson: May 44–Jun 44)*, Canadian Casualty Evac. Flt. *(Dakota: Dec 44–Jan 45)*.

CROYDON – 1 *(JX: Hurricane: Apr 41–May 41)*, 2 AC *(KO: Lysander: May 40)*, 3 *(QO: Hurricane: Sep 39–Oct 39)*, 17 *(YB: Hurricane: Sep 39)*, 85 *(YO: Hurricane: Aug 40–Sep 40)*, 92 *(GR: Blenheim, Spitfire: Dec 39–May 40)*, 111 *(JU: Hurricane: Jun 40–Aug 40, Sep 40)*, 116 *(II: Oxford: Jul 42–Jul 44)*, 145 *(SO: Blenheim, Hurricane: Oct 39–Apr 40)*, 287 AC *(KZ: Blenheim, Lysander, Oxford, Hurricane, Hudson, Defiant, Master: Jun 41–Jul 44)*, 302 *(WX: Spitfire: Jun 42–Jul 42)*, 317 *(JU: Spitfire: Jun 42–Jul 42)*, 401 *(YO: Hurricane: Jul 40–Aug 40)*, 414 AC *(RU: Lysander, Tomahawk, Mustang: Aug 41–Dec 42)*, 501 *(SD: Hurricane: Jun 40–Jul 40)*, 605 *(UP: Hurricane:*

Sep 40–Feb 41), 607 *(AF: Gladiator: Nov 39, May 40–Jun 40)*, 615 *(DW: Gladiator: Sep 39)*, 1 Delivery Flt. *(Dominie: Jul 42)*, 110 Wing Transport Comm. *(Dakota: 1943)*.

KENLEY – 1 *(JX: Hurricane: Jan 41–Apr 41, Jun 41)*, 3 *(QO: Hurricane: Aug 36–May 39, Jan 40–May 40, May 40)*, 17 *(UV: Hurricane: May 40–Jun 40)*, 64 *(SH: Spitfire: May 40–Aug 40)*, 66 *(LZ: Spitfire: Sep 40, Aug 43–Sep 43)*, 111 *(JU: Spitfire: Jul 42–Sep 42)*, 165 *(SK: Spitfire: Aug 43–Sep 43)*, 253 *(SW: Hurricane: May 40)*, 258 *(ZT: Hurricane: Apr 41–Jun 41)*, 302 *(WX: Hurricane: Apr 41–May 41)*, 312 *(DU: Hurricane: May 41–Jul 41)*, 350 *(MN: Spitfire: Jul 42)*, 401 *(YO: Spitfire: Sep 42–Jan 43)*, 402 *(AE: Spitfire: May 42, Aug 42–Mar 43)*, 403 *(KH: Spitfire: Jan 43–Aug 43, Oct 43–Feb 44, Feb 44–Apr 44)*, 411 *(DB: Spitfire: Mar 43–Apr 43)*, 412 *(VZ: Spitfire: Nov 42)*, 416 *(DN: Spitfire: Feb 43–May 43, Feb 44–Apr 44)*, 421 *(AU: Spitfire: Jan 43–Mar 43, Mar 43, May 43–Aug 43, Oct 43–Feb 44)*, 452 *(NI: Spitfire: Jul 41–Oct 41, Jan 42–Apr 42)*, 485 *(OU: Spitfire: Oct 41–Jul 42)*, 501 *(SD: Hurricane: Sep 40–Dec 40)*, 602 *(LO: Spitfire: Jul 41–Jan 42, Mar 42–May 42)*, 611 *(FY: Spitfire: Jun 42–Jul 42)*, 615 *(KW: Gladiator, Hurricane: Sep 38–Sep 39, May 40–Aug 40, Dec 40–Apr 41)*, 616 *(YQ: Spitfire: Aug 40–Sep 40, Jul 42)*.

FAIROAKS – 18 EFTS *(Tiger Moth, Hind, Audax: Sep 39–May 47)*.

GATWICK – 2 *(XV: Mustang: Apr 44–Jun 44)*, 4 *(FY: Spitfire, Mosquito: Apr 44–Jun 44)*, 18 *(May 40–Jun 40)*, 26 AC *(Lysander, Tomahawk, Mustang: Sep 40–Jul 43)*, 57 *(DX: Blenheim: Jun 40–Jul 40)*, 65 *(YT: Spitfire: Oct 43)*, 80 *(W2: Spitfire: Jun 44–Aug 44)*, 98 *(Battle: Jul 40)*, 116 *(II: Anson, Oxford: Aug 44)*, 122 *(MT: Spitfire: Oct 43)*, 141 *(TW: Defiant: Oct 40–Nov 40)*, 168 *(QC: Typhoon: Mar 44)*, 171 *(Tomahawk, Mustang: Apr 42–Jul 42, Aug 42–Dec 42)*, 175 *(HH: Hurricane: Dec 42–Jan 43)*, 183 *(HF: Typhoon: Mar 43–May 43)*, 229 *(9R: Spitfire: Jun 44–Jul 44)*, 239 AC *(HB: Lysander, Tomahawk, Hurricane, Mustang: Oct 40–Aug 42, Jan 43–Jun 43)*, 268 AC *(Mustang: Apr 40–Jun 40)*, 274 *(JJ: Spitfire: Jun 44–Jul 44)*, 309 AC *(Mustang: Dec 42–Jan 43)*, 400 AC *(Mustang: Aug 42, Nov 43–Feb 44)*, 414 AC *(Mustang: Aug 42, Jul 43–Aug 43, Nov 43–Feb 44, Feb 44–Mar 44)*, 430 AC *(Tomahawk, Mustang: Jul 43–Aug 43, Oct 43–Apr 44)*, 655 AOP *(Auster: Mar 43–Apr 43)*, 83 Gp. Comm. Sq. *(Anson, Oxford etc: Nov 45–)*, 84 Gp. Comm. Sq. *(Anson, Oxford etc: Aug 43–Feb 44, Nov 45–)*, 85 Gp. Comm. Sq. *(Anson, Oxford etc: Mar 45–)*.

HORNE – 130 *(AP: Spitfire: Apr 44–Jun 44)*, 303 *(RF: Spitfire: Apr 44–Jun 44)*, 402 *(AE: Spitfire: Apr 44–Jun 44)*.

COBHAM – 110 AC RCAF *(Lysander: Sep 40)*, 652 AOP *(Auster: Apr 44–May 44)*.

FAIRCHILDS FARM – 661 AOP *(Auster: Feb 44–July 44)*.

GLOSSARY

Types of operations carried out and fighter escorts:

ARTILLERY RANGING	– Arty/R. Spotting for guns. Flying over the target and directing fire.
CIRCUS	– Heavy fighter escorts to small forces of day bombers attacking short range targets, the prime object being to draw enemy fighters up to attack
CLOSE ESCORT	– Surrounding bombers
ESCORT COVER	– Cover for close escort fighters
HIGH COVER	– To prevent enemy fighters positioning themselves above the close and escort cover
JIM CROW	– Patrols of the home coastline to intercept any enemy aircraft crossing the coast; also to spot invasion forces
POPULAR	– Small-scale photo or tactical reconnaissance, limited to coastal areas
RAMROD	– Similar to Circus operations but destruction of the target the primary aim
RANGER	– Freelance intrusion of large force of fighters over enemy territory to wear out the fighter defence
RHUBARB	– Small-scale fighter or fighter-bomber attacks on targets of opportunity
ROADSTEAD	– Codename for attacks by dive-bombing or low level attack on shipping at sea or in harbour by fighters or bombers escorted by fighters
RODEO	– Fighter sweeps over enemy territory
TACTICAL RECONNAISANCE	– Tac/R. Reconnaisance of specific areas; searching, observing, photographing. Often at low-level, by pairs of aircraft.
TOP COVER	– Roving commission, but tied to bombers en route to sweep skies near to target.

ACKNOWLEDGEMENTS

I am extremely grateful to all the organisations and individuals who gave their assistance in the writing of this book.

The Imperial War Museum, Public Records Office, Surrey Record Office, British Aerospace, BAA Gatwick, Mike Goodall of Brooklands Museum, Major John Cross of The Museum of Army Flying, John Janaway of Surrey Local Studies at Guildford, Kathleen Shawcross of Sutton Heritage Service, Allan Hopkins of Bristow Helicopters, Mr G. I. Smith of The 615 Squadron Association, *The Croydon Advertiser*, *The Surrey Herald*, *The Surrey Mirror*, *The Surrey Advertiser*.

H. Failes, Mrs D. Fairhead, P. Stock, Mrs M. Munt, Mr N. Dunne, A. Johnson, and many others who kindly responded to the author's appeal for information.

I would particularly like to thank the following people: Air Commodore P. M. Brothers for his Redhill reminiscences, Sir Peter Masefield for his help in the history of Surrey airfields, Roger Jackson for the loan of the A. J. Jackson Collection photographs of the late C. Nepean Bishop, John King for help with Gatwick and Redhill and photographs, Geoff Tait for help with Gatwick and *Redhill at War*, Alfred Price for his help with wartime Kenley and *The Hardest Day*, Alan Milton for his valuable help with wartime Fairoaks and photographs, Brian Buss for his wartime and postwar reminiscences of Redhill and for generous help with the history and photographs of RAF Horne, Rex Nicholls for wartime reminiscences and help with Croydon and Redhill, Paul McCue for use of his Dunsfold notes and a fine set of photos, Dave Collyer, KAHRS archivist, for the loan of many photographs, Peter Flint, a great help with Kenley's history and photographs, Frank Cheesman for his wealth of aviation history and photographs, Chaz Bowyer and Bruce Robertson for assistance with photographs, Chris Elliott for his help with Kenley and for the loan of photographs and Luftwaffe target maps, and Vickers plc for use of photographs.

Lastly, my grateful thanks to Robin Brooks for his great help and encouragement in writing this book.

L.P.

BIBLIOGRAPHY

During my research I consulted various books and publications. I list them below with grateful thanks to the authors.

Andrews, C. F. & Morgan, E. B., *Vickers Aircraft*, Putnam 1988
Ashmore, E. B., *Air Defence*, Longmans Green, 1929
Ashworth, Chris, *Action Stations 9*, Patrick Stephenson Ltd
Bowyer, Chaz, *The Wellington Bomber*, William Kimber 1986
Bowyer, M. J. F., *Action Stations 1*, Patrick Stephens Ltd
Bowyer, M. J. F., *Battle of Britain*, Patrick Stephens 1990
Buss, Brian, *RAF Horne's D-Day Spitfires*, B. Buss 1994
Cluett, Douglas, Bogle, Joanna & Learmouth, Bob, *Croydon Airport in the Battle for Britain*, Sutton Libraries & Arts Services
Collyer, D., *Buzz Bomb Diary*, Kent Aviation & Historical Research Society 1994
Darlington, Roger, *Nighthawk*, William Kimber 1985
Dunne, Nigel *The Redhill Story*, D. Canning Redhill 1950
Flint, Peter, *RAF Kenley*, Terence Dalton 1985
Halpenny, Bruce Barry, *Action Stations 8*, Patrick Stephens Ltd
Hough, Richard & Richards, Denis, *Battle of Britain*, Hodder & Stoughton 1989
Humphreys, Roy, *RAF Hawkinge*, Meresborough Books 1981
Johnson, Howard, *Wings Over Brooklands*, Whittet Books
Johnson, Gp Capt J., *Wing Leader*, Chatto & Windus 1956
King, John & Tait, Geoff, *Golden Gatwick*, Royal Aeronautical Society/ BAA
Liskutin, S., *Challenge in the Air*, William Kimber 1988
Masefield, Sir Peter, *Surrey Aeronautics and Aviation 1785–1985*, Phillimore
McCue, P., *Dunsfold, Surrey's Most Secret Airfield*, Air Research
Ogley, Bob, *Surrey At War*, Froglets Publications Ltd
Pile, Gen. Sir Frederick, *Ack-Ack*
Price, Alfred, *Battle of Britain – The Hardest Day*, McDonald Janes 1979
Price, Alfred, *Instruments of Darkness*, McDonald Janes 1977
Quill, Jeffrey, *Spitfire – A Test Pilot's Story*, John Murrey 1983
Quill, Jeffrey, *Birth Of A Legend*, Quiller Press Ltd 1986
Rawlings, John D., *Fighter Squadrons of the RAF*, McDonald 1969
Sayers, Berwick, *Croydon in the Second World War*

Shores, Christopher F., *2nd Tactical Air Force*, Osprey 1970
Surrey Record Office, *Special Report of the Special War Executive Comm. 1945*
Tait, Geoff & Smith, Paul, *Redhill At War, The Lighter Side*, G. Tait Associates
Townsend, Peter, *Duel Of Eagles*, Cassells 1970
Wells, Kevin, *Illustrated History of No. 485 Squadron RNZAF*

Public Record Office:
During my research I consulted various documents, operation record books and squadron logs listed below, which are Crown Copyright and published by kind permission of the Controller of HMSO.

Operation record books: RAF Kenley (Air 28/419); RAF Croydon (Air 28/178); RAF Redhill (Air 28/667); RAF Dunsfold (Air 28/231); RAF Gatwick (Air 28/257); 15 ERFTS Redhill (Air 29/619); 18 ERFTS Fairoaks (Air 29/619).
Squadron records: No 1 (Air 27/1); No 4 (Air 27/47); No 26 (Air 27/317); No 83; No 85 (Air 27/703); No 98 (Air 27/781/7); No 111 (Air 27/866); No 145 (Air 27/984); No 239 (Air 27/14566); No 287 (Air 27/1622/3); No 317 (Air 27/1706/10); No 400 (Air 27/1770); No 401 (Air 27/1771/4); No 414 (Air 27/1803/7); No 430 (Air 27/1856); No 501 (Air 27/1949); No 607 (Air 27/2093); No 615 (Air 27/2123); No 652 (Air 27/2170); No 661 (Air 27/2187).
Airfield site plans of RAF Horne, Kenley, Redhill, Gatwick, Dunsfold, Croydon, and Fairoaks (Air 28/4039).

INDEX